Your Ultimate Guide to Implementing PKI

Calvin Yap

Copyright © 2023 by Calvin Yap
All rights reserved worldwide.
First Edition 2023

Some of the information from this book was obtained from the Internet. Acknowledgement is given to the authors and/or creator of Wikipedia and Google in general. Any omission of acknowledgement is unintentional. Please inform the author so that such acknowledgement can be included in the next edition. All other intellectual property rights contained or in relation to this book belong to Calvin Yap.

No part of this book may be copied, used, reproduced, or transmitted in any form or by any means, graphic, electronic, or mechanical, including photocopying, recording, taping or by any information storage or retrieval system, without the permission in writing from the author.

The author can be reached at:
Email: Calvin Yap (calvin.yap@knittechnologies.com)
Website: http://www.knittechnologies.com/

Cover Design / Edited by: Crystal Loh

Contents

Figures

About The Author

Calvin Yap is one of the pioneers of PKI in Singapore, having introduced it in the 90s. He still remembers being interviewed by the Internal Security Department (ISD) when attempting to import PKI software, which was then classified as ammunition. He also played a key role in Netrust achieving its first cross-certification with the Canadian government using X.500 directory technology. For the past decade, he has been involved in designing, building, and managing PKI infrastructures for classified customers in Singapore, leading a team of security-cleared staff in implementing and operating PKI infrastructure for classified projects in Singapore. Calvin also spearheaded the adoption of PIV in the Singapore government and defence.

In his spare time, Calvin is an internationally recognized Fengshui Master, having published over 20 books on Fengshui-related topics. Due to COVID-19, all his courses are currently conducted via distance learning.

About KNIT

Knit Technologies was established to bridge cyber security needs by bringing people, process, and technology together. The company provides high-quality implementation, management, and consultancy services for cyber security projects. The company comprises cyber security experts who have vast experiences in cyber security and have implemented multi-million-dollar projects in their previous roles for customers in various industries covering both public and commercial sectors.

Some of the staff that are currently with Knit Technologies are led by the author in implementing and managing classified PKI projects in Singapore in their previous tenure together and were personally mentored by him.

Public Key Infrastructure (PKI) Market

PKI was "invented" in 1976 and began to see widespread adoption in 1994. At the height of the PKI boom, companies like Baltimore were FTSE 100 firms with thousands of employees and a market capitalization of over US $13 billion. When Baltimore was acquired by Oryx International Growth Fund in July 2006, it had only a scant 12 employees. In the end, the "year of PKI" as predicted by Gartner failed to materialize.

However, PKI is still very much alive today. If you look around, all websites that use SSL have certificates that are issued from a PKI system. Additionally, all company-wide deployments of IPsec-based VPNs use certificates issued by either a private PKI or commercial PKI system. In the paper "***Evaluating SSL Certificates for E-Business***" published on August 30th, 2011, Gartner stated that through 2016, SSL digital certificates will remain a commoditized offering by PKI systems.

On April 13th, 2010, Gartner published a paper titled "Goldilocks and the Case for PKI or PKO," which outlined some key findings:

- The most common reason that many public-key systems fail is the lack of direct correlation between requirements and the configured public-key system.
- Organizations continue to struggle with the implementation of public-key systems for internal and external

deployments due to their persistent lack of understanding of basic design principles, real-world requirements, and deployment philosophies.

- Organizations typically attempt to design and implement public-key systems for maximum flexibility and applicability instead of maximum simplicity and effectiveness, resulting in a significantly high cost of operation and support.

This means that the implementation of PKI fails in most organizations because the organization tries to build a "buffet of PKI services" and expects users (internal or external) to subscribe to the services. What is really required is a PKI system that is specifically built based on the user's requirements. In this way, there will be solid and strong business cases with well-defined ROI to ensure the sustainability of the PKI system. This term is being coined as Public Key Operation or PKO by Gartner.

How PKI works.

Peter Steiner's cartoon, as published in *The New Yorker* on July 5, 1993

The PKI system is based on a system of trusted third parties. In this system, there is a third party that everybody trusts (called the Certification Authority or CA in PKI terms). It is the same analogy as an Immigration Authority that issues a passport to an individual. Any foreign authority will have to trust the passport issued by the Immigration Authority when a person presents the passport at the immigration counter. Hence, the Immigration Authority that issues the passport becomes the trusted third party.

A Public Key Infrastructure (PKI) enables asymmetric cryptography to be used to satisfy many types of requirements for authentication, confidentiality, and non-repudiation.

PKI Components

The diagram below shows the general components of PKI:

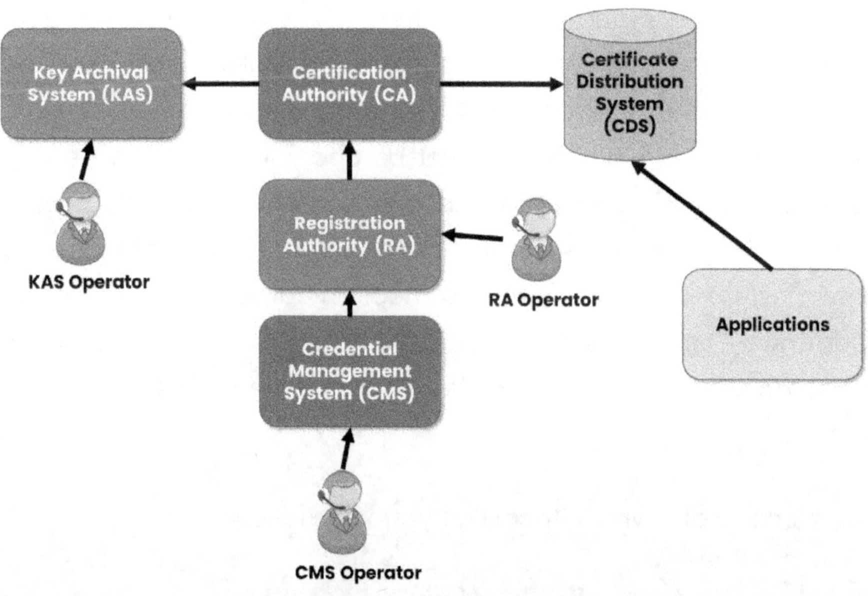

Figure 1- PKI Component

Basic usage of PKI

The basic usage of PKI is to provide the following security controls:

- Authentication
- Confidentiality
- Non-Repudiation

There are two types of encryptions being used in the PKI world. The first is called Symmetric Encryption, where the same key is used for both encryption and decryption. The second type is called Asymmetric Encryption, where different keys are used for both encryption and decryption. These keys are called Public Key and Private Key, respectively. In Asymmetric Encryption, if data is encrypted with Public Key, it must be decrypted with Private Key. Likewise, if data is encrypted with Private Key, it must be decrypted with Public Key. Public Key can be distributed freely, but the Private Key must be stored in a secured medium called a Security Token. Commonly used Security Tokens are Smart Cards, Secured USBs (e.g., YubiKey), Secure SD cards, Secure Elements like TPM Chips, etc.

An overview of Asymmetrical Encryption as follow:

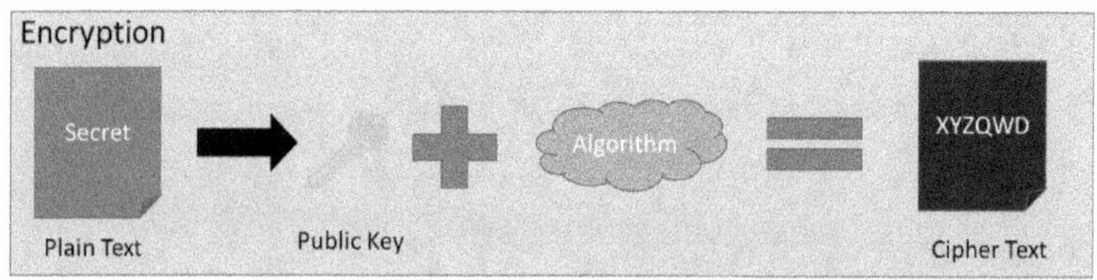

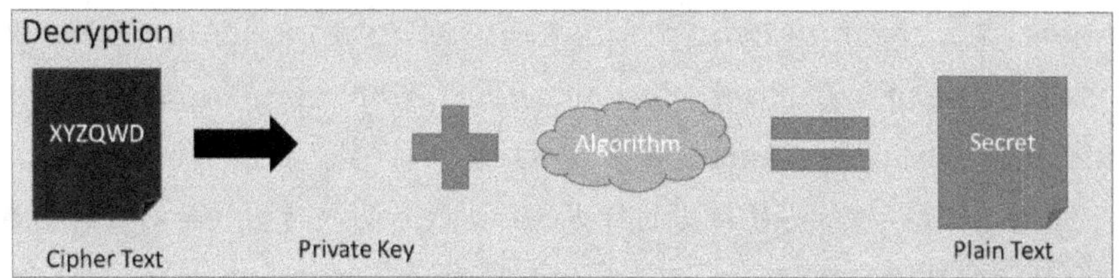

Figure 2- Asymmetrical Encryption

Authentication

Authentication is the process of proving or demonstrating that something is true, genuine, or valid. Authentication follows identification, which involves presenting an ID or some other form of identification, and the authentication process confirms the claim made by the person or system.

The most common use of PKI authentication is server-side SSL validation. When you access a website using the HTTPS protocol, your browser authenticates the site you are visiting to ensure that it is legitimate. For example, when your browser accesses the DBS website, **https://www.dbs.com.sg/**, the DBS web server presents a certificate issued by a trusted Certification Authority (CA) to prove its identity. The trusted CA is already pre-trusted in every browser (as a trusted third party), and when the DBS web server presents the certificate, your browser can verify that the site is indeed trustworthy. If the site is trustworthy, your browser will display a lock icon.

Another common usage of PKI for authentication is the deployment of 2-factor authentication (2FA) using security tokens like Smart Card or Secure USB. This is where the user's certificate and private key are stored in the security token. The security token is protected by a PIN or password. When a system requests 2FA authentication, the user plugs in the security token and unlocks it with the PIN or password. This satisfies the 2FA requirement where having the security token is "what you have" and entering the PIN is "what you know."

In the underlying architecture, the system that authenticates the user sends the user a time-sensitive digital token, and the user encrypts this digital token using the user's private key stored in the security token. The encrypted information is sent to the authentication system where the encrypted information is decrypted with the user's public key. Once the information is decrypted, this proves the identity of the user. This function is called Digital Signature or Non-Repudiation.

Confidentiality

Confidentiality aims to protect data and ensure that only the intended recipient can access it. Encryption is used to achieve confidentiality, as mentioned earlier. Two methods can be used to ensure confidentiality, Symmetrical or Asymmetrical encryption. Symmetrical encryption is faster and uses fewer processing resources, but there are challenges in protecting the key. This is similar to the key to your door, you need to ensure that you do not drop it, as anyone who finds it can open your door. On the other hand, Asymmetrical encryption is slower and requires more resources to process, but it addresses the key protection issue. The Private Key must be kept secure, while the Public Key can be distributed freely.

Therefore, if Alice wants to share something with Bob and ensure confidentiality, she will encrypt the data with Bob's Public Key and send it to him. To view the data, Bob must decrypt it with his Private Key. This ensures that only Bob can access the data.

Non-Repudiation

Non-repudiation ensures that someone cannot deny the validity of something, which is commonly achieved through Digital Signature. It is similar to signing a contract to provide assurance that the information is correct. In PKI, the process involves encrypting the data with the sender's Private Key. When the recipient receives the encrypted data, they decrypt it using the sender's Public Key (which is readily available and widely distributed). The recipient can be assured that the data is sent by the sender because only the sender's Public Key can be used to decrypt the data.

Certification Authority (CA)

The Certification Authority or CA is the ultimate system that is going to sign the certificate request. The CA receives the certificate signing request (CSR) in the form of PKCS#10 format. The CA then signs the CSR with its private key to form the full X.509 certificate.

There are many ways to build the Certification Authority. It can be built in a flat architecture or hierarchical architecture. A flat architecture will have a single Certification Authority that will sign all requests.

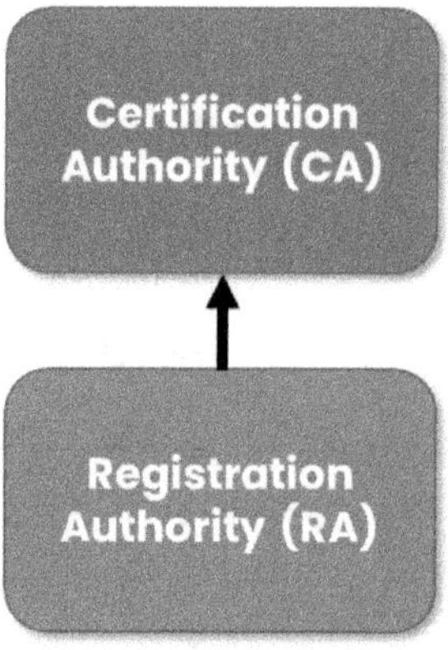

Figure 3-Single tier CA

However, some customers prefer to have a multi-tier architecture as follows. The main purpose of having a multi-tier architecture is defence-in-depth. If an Intermediate Certification Authority (ICA) is compromised, there is still a Root CA to sign a new ICA and start issuing certificates.

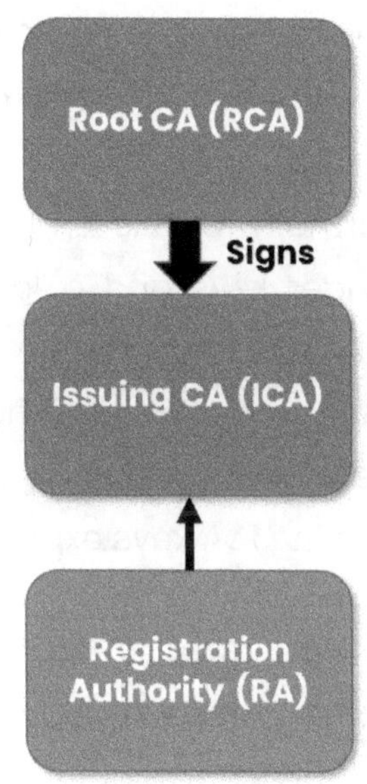

Figure 4–2 tier CA.

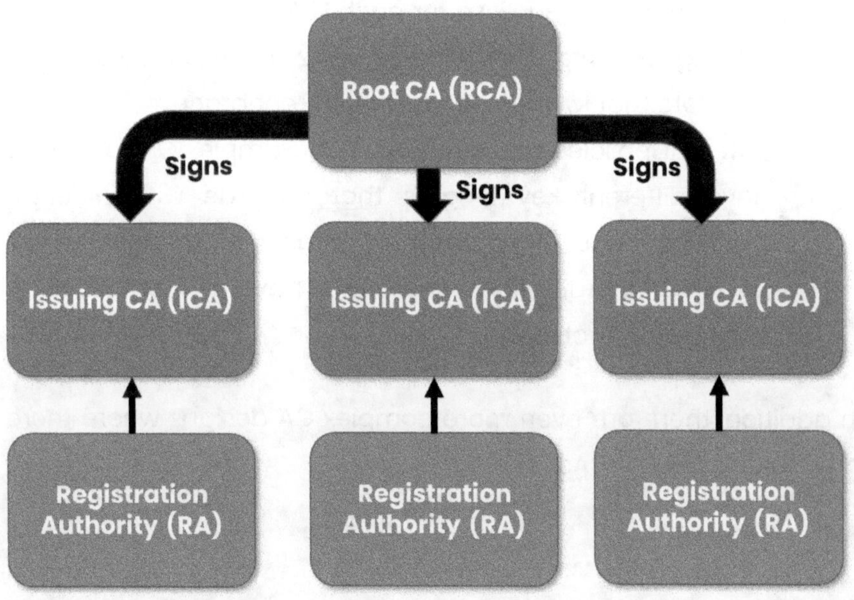

Figure 5- Single Root - Multiple ICAs

For a 2-**tier CA**, the Root CA will sign the ICA CSR to form a tiered CA. Normally in this case, the Root CA shall be shut down after the signing is complete. The ICA will continue to service all requests from RA to sign CSR. Normally for this kind of implementation, the Root CA will have stronger keys and a longer lifespan (e.g., 20 years). The ICA will have lesser key strength and a shorter lifespan. The main purpose of such a design is to have trust anchored at the Root CA level, where a new ICA can be created to replace the existing ICA when the existing ICA keys expire or are compromised.

For a **Single Root – Multiple ICAs** structure, a single Root CA will sign multiple ICAs. The main purpose of having multiple ICAs is:

- Segregation of duties for different divisions or departments, where each division or department manages their own ICA.
- Different usage purpose for each ICA. For example, ICA1 for signing of servers' certificates, ICA2 for users' certificates, etc. Note that ICAs can be from different brands.
- Different policies and liabilities. For example, ICA1 and ICA2 have different key lengths that coincide with different liabilities. This is a normal practice in commercial Certification Authorities where they have different levels of liability and protection.

In addition, there are even more complex CA designs where there are multiple tiers of CAs:

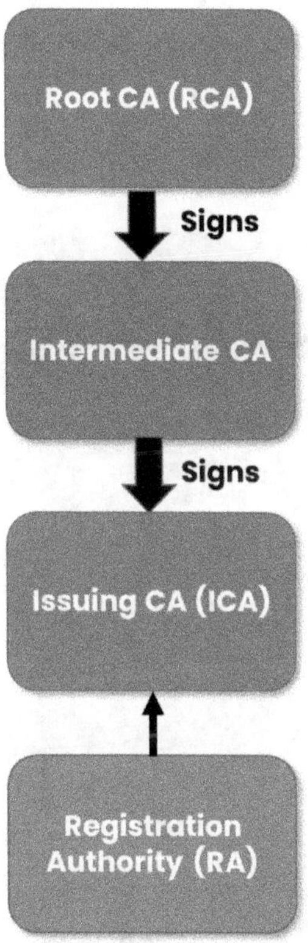

Figure 6- multiple tier CAs

This **multiple-tier CAs** model is mainly used in global MNCs where their headquarters will maintain the Root CA, and each region will manage the Intermediate CA, followed by each branch office having its own Issuing CA.

Strategies you can consider

Which model to choose mainly depends on the policies and needs of the company. However, it's important to note that the more Certification Authorities you have, the more hardware and security controls are required. In addition, companies need to take into consideration defence-in-depth and risk level when deciding on the level of Certification Authority, whether it's vertical or horizontal.

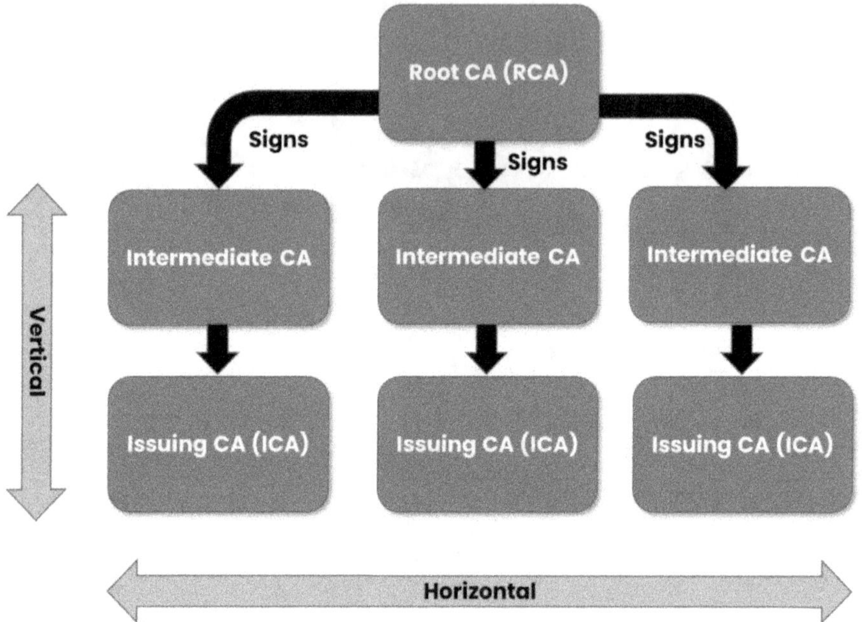

Figure 7- Vertical or Horizontal?

Multiple issuing CAs can be used for large corporations to provide segregation of controls. For example, each division can have its own Certification Authority and PKI operation team to manage. Multiple intermediate Certification Authorities can be used to mitigate the risk of CA compromise. For example, if one of the intermediate CA keys is compromised, other intermediate CAs can continue to operate. On the other hand, if there is a single Certification Authority and its keys are compromised, then the entire PKI must be revoked, and a new PKI system has to be set up. When deciding on the number of Certification Authorities to use, companies need to take into consideration their policies, needs, and level of risk. Note that the more Certification Authorities there are, the more hardware and security controls are required, so companies must also factor in the costs and resources needed for this.

Registration Authority (RA)

The Registration Authority (RA) function is to perform certificate enrolment requests, validate the requests before sending the certificate signing request (CSR) to the Certification Authority (CA) for signing, and manage certificate revocation requests before sending them to the CA for revocation. The purpose of the Registration Authority is to offload the function from the CA so that the CA can concentrate on certificate signing and revocation.

By design, you can have multiple RAs connecting to a single CA. Using the Post Office as an example, you can have an RA in every Post Office branch that connects to a single CA in HQ.

For example, if a user wants a certificate, he/she will approach a Registration Authority Operator (RAO), who will verify the person's identity and generate the certificate request. Once the certificate is signed by the CA, the RAO shall provide the certificate to the requester via any approved means. This could be a smart card, USB token, or mobile phone app.

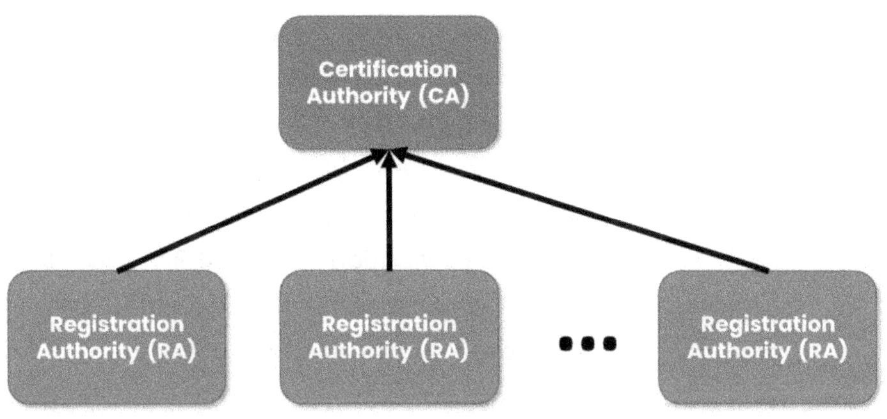

Figure 8- Registration Authority

The Registration Authority is also used to interface with any certificate automation request as follow:

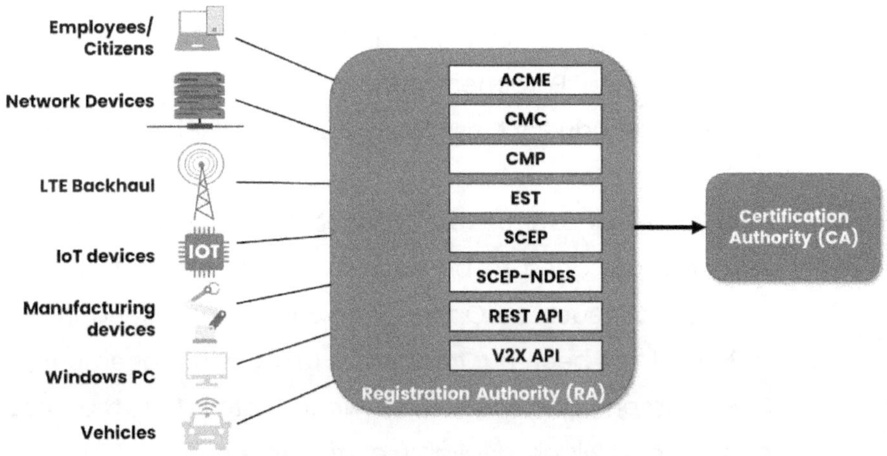

Figure 9- Certificate processing

- ACME, *Automated Certificate Management Environment*, is a protocol that makes it possible to automate the issuance of certificates without human interaction. The first interaction of the ACME protocol, ACME v1, was released in 2016 and initially only supported the issuance of certificates for only one domain. The updated ACME v2, released in 2018, supports the issuance of wildcard certificates and better domain ownership verification. In 2019, the IETF standardized the ACME protocol in RFC8555, and the V1 protocol was deprecated entirely in June 2021.

- CMC, *Certificate Management over CMS*, is an internet standard published by the IETF defining transport mechanisms for the Cryptographic Message Syntax (CMS). It is defined in RFC 5272, and the transport mechanism is defined in RFC 5273.

- CMP, *Certificate Management Protocol*, is an Internet protocol standardized by the IETF used for obtaining X.509 digital certificates in a PKI environment. CMP is described in RFC 4210. The Enrolment request messages employ the Certificate Request Message Format (CRMF) described in RFC 4211.

- EST, *Enrolment over Secure Transport*, the basic functions of EST were designed to be easy to use and REST-like using simple tools such as OpenSSL or cURL. It is defined in RFC 7030 and has been put forward as an SCEP replacement.

- SCEP, *Simple Certificate Enrolment Protocol*, is the most popular and widely available certificate enrolment protocol being used by numerous network equipment manufacturers which provides a simplified means of handling certificates for large-scale implementation. SCEP is defined in RFC 8894.

- SCEP-NDES, *SCEP-Network Device Enrolment Service*, is the Microsoft implementation of the SCEP protocol. SCEP-NDES is used to enrol non-AD joined devices, appliances, switches, and routers. It is mainly used for Microsoft Mobile Device Management (MDM) to facilitate MDM-based certificate enrolment and provisioning.

- REST API, RESTful API is an interface that two computer systems use to exchange information securely over the internet. Representational State Transfer (REST) is a software architecture that imposes conditions on how an API should work. REST was initially created as a guideline to manage communication on a complex network like the internet. You can use REST-based architecture to support high-performing and reliable communication at scale. An application programming interface (API) defines the rules that you must follow to communicate with other software systems. Developers expose or create APIs so that other applications can communicate with their applications programmatically. REST API is widely used on the Internet for machine-to-machine communications.

- V2X API, Vehicle-to-Everything API, is an Abstract Syntax Notation One (ASN.1) API that supports the encoding and decoding of data in ASN.1 unaligned-PER (U-PER) format as defined in SAE J2735, ETSI EN 302 637-2, ETSI EN 302 637-3, and ETSI TS 103 301. It provides messages encoded between PER and JSON/XML. (JSON=JavaScript Object Notation, XML=Extensible Markup Language) This protocol allows automotive to perform certificate management with a PKI system.

Strategies you can consider

Before deciding on the number of Registration Authorities (RAs), you need to have a clear strategy for the purpose of the PKI. For example, for large multinational corporations (MNCs) deploying user certificates, you will need at least one RA to be deployed in every office to manage the certificate lifecycle of the users. For issuing certificates to devices, you will need a separate RA to manage their certificate lifecycle.

In addition, the protocol used for certificate management must be taken into consideration, as not all protocols are supported by some Certification Authority brands.

Finally, there are also staffing requirements for the Registration Authority Operators (RAOs) and verification processes for them to follow.

Hardware Security Module (HSM)

The sole function of the Hardware Security Module (HSM) is to safeguard keys as PKI keys are the crown jewels of the entire PKI system. If the PKI keys are compromised or stolen, it will render the entire PKI system useless. During the setup of PKI, the Certification Authority keys are generated in the HSM and the Private Key is stored in the HSM. Only the Public Key of the Certification Authority is published on the Certification Distribution System (CDS), and the Private Key is used to sign any certificate request. The Private Key will forever stay inside the HSM and be backed up in encrypted form.

Type of HSM

There are two types of HSMs in the market: PKI HSM and payment HSM. PKI HSMs are used for PKI purposes, while payment HSMs are used for payment transactions like ATM and credit card transactions.

HSM Security

All HSMs have a tamper-resistant module where all the protected keys are stored. This tamper resistance is to ensure that the keys are secure. When an HSM detects any attempt to steal the key (i.e., tamper), the HSM will destroy all the keys. Depending on the brand of HSM, some HSMs will reset the entire system to factory settings, and some will require a return to the factory to reset. At this stage, the HSM backup shall be recalled and used to restore the backup keys into the HSM.

The most commonly accepted standard for HSM tamper resistance certification is under the National Institute of Standards and Technology (NIST) Federal Information Processing Standards (FIPS) 140. As of October 2020, both FIPS 140-2 and FIPS 140-3 are current and active. FIPS 140-3 was approved on March 22, 2019, as the successor to FIPS 140-2 and became effective on September 22, 2019. FIPS 140-3 testing began on September 22, 2020, although no FIPS 140-3 validation certificates have been issued yet as of writing. FIPS 140-2 testing is still available until September 21, 2021 (later changed for applications already in progress to April 1, 2022), creating an overlapping transition period of one year.

FIPS 140 imposes requirements in eleven areas:

1. Cryptographic module specification
2. Cryptographic module ports and interfaces
3. Roles, services and authentication
4. Finite state model
5. Physical security
6. Operational environment
7. Cryptographic key management
8. Electromagnetic Interference /Electromagnetic Compatibility
9. Self-tests
10. Design assurance
11. Mitigation of other attacks

FIPS 140-2 defines four levels of security, simply named "Level 1" to "Level 4".

- FIPS 140-2 Level 1 is the lowest level and imposes very limited requirements; all components must be "production-grade," and various egregious kinds of insecurity must be absent.
- FIPS 140-2 Level 2 adds requirements for physical tamper-evidence and role-based authentication.
- FIPS 140-2 Level 3 adds requirements for physical tamper-resistance (making it difficult for attackers to gain access to sensitive information contained in the module) and identity-based authentication, and for a physical or logical separation between the interfaces by which "critical security parameters" enter and leave the module and its other interfaces.
- FIPS 140-2 Level 4 makes the physical security requirements more stringent and requires robustness against environmental attacks.

In the market, the most common HSM are certified on Level 2 or Level 3. There are limited HSM in the market that is certified on Level 4.

HSM Backup

To ensure availability, the keys stored in the HSM are backed up to external devices like smart cards or USB thumb drives. As an added security measure, the backup is split into multiple parts to ensure that no single person holds the complete key. This is done by using m of n permutation, with the most common permutation being *2 of 4*, although some use *3 of 6* or *4 of 8*.

In the *2 of 4* permutation, the keys are backed up into 4 packages, which are then distributed to 4 separate individuals for secure storage. To restore the keys back to the HSM, any 2 out of the 4 people must retrieve their packages and combine them to restore the keys. Similarly, for the *3 of 6* permutation, 6 packages are generated and distributed to 6 people, and any 3 of them must retrieve their packages to restore the keys.

The entire process of generating the relevant keys in the HSM and backing up (or restoring) the keys is called a Key Ceremony. Once the package is generated, it is handed over to the assigned individuals for safekeeping, who are known as Key Custodians.

HSM virtual partition and high availability

Due to the high cost of HSM hardware, some HSM brands provide virtual partition features. This allows a single physical HSM to be partitioned and used by multiple systems. The operation is similar to using individual physical HSMs, except they are housed in a single physical chassis. The operation for each virtual partition is the same as for a physical HSM.

Most HSM brands support high availability setups. However, depending on the brand implementation, some HSMs use "software high availability" instead of "hardware high availability."

In the "software high availability" model, a software sits in front of the clustered HSM and performs key duplications to the HSM clusters. When one of the HSMs fails and is replaced, the keys are not automatically restored to the new HSM. You need to manually backup and restore the keys from the existing HSM to the new HSM.

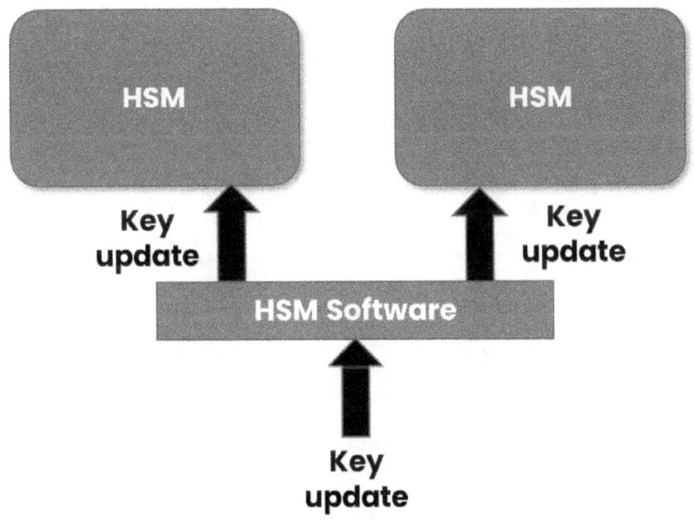

Figure 10- Software HA

Some brand of HSM implemented the "hardware high availability" where keys are synchronised between the HSMs.

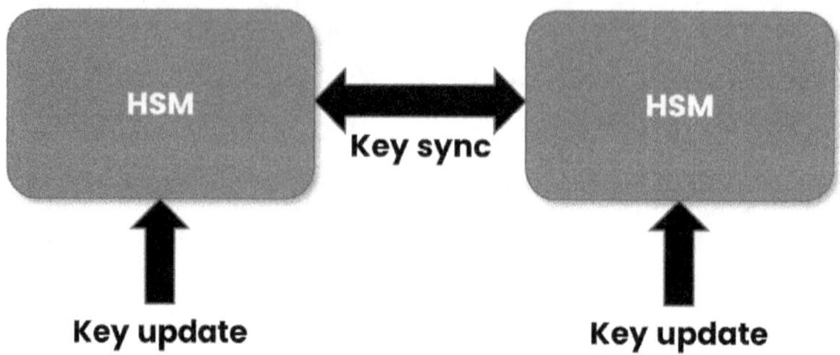

Figure 11- Hardware HA

In this setup, any update made to a key in any of the HSMs will automatically synchronize the key between the HSMs in the group. As long as all the HSMs are configured as a group, all the keys will be synchronized across all the HSMs. If one of the HSMs fails, a new HSM can be configured to join the group. The keys will then be automatically synchronized to the new HSM.

HSM Operation

In the context of PKI, HSMs are critical for protecting the crown jewels, and are extremely sensitive to the physical environment, especially those that meet FIPS-140 level 4 requirements. Therefore, HSMs need a steady stream of power and an isothermal environment. Any fluctuations in power or temperature could cause the HSM to suspect an attack and destroy all the keys, which is the tamper-resistance mechanism of the HSM.

Furthermore, all HSMs have internal batteries to ensure that all the keys are maintained when power is off. However, due to the limitations of lithium batteries, they begin to deplete between the

4th and 5th year of manufacturing. As a rule of thumb, HSM batteries must be replaced after the 5th year of operation. If not, once the battery is depleted, all the keys will be destroyed. Therefore, having a good backup strategy is crucial.

When starting up the PKI system, as a security best practice, the HSM services should be started manually to ensure that the operation is legitimate. If the HSM services are started automatically, a hacker could power off the HSM, steal it, power it on again in another location, and begin impersonating the PKI system.

Some HSM brands have a dual control mechanism, where the physical HSM is a passive device, and a separate physical management device is used to manage all the HSMs. Once the HSM services are started, the management device can be locked up. Additionally, the associated smart cards for HSM operation can only be operated via the management device. This provides added security controls for the HSM operation.

Crypto currencies HSM

Some HSM brands support various crypto currencies protocols like Bitcoin, XRP, Ethereum, EOS, Tether, Litecoin, TRON, Stellar, Cardano, Binance Coin, Monero, IOTA, Dash, NEO, Tezos, VeChain or Zcash. If there is a business requirement, then having an HSM that supports crypto currencies will provide added security.

HSM as a service

Some HSM brands provide HSM on the cloud service. Instead of owning and having a secure space for the in-house HSM, customers can subscribe to the HSM on the cloud service operated by either the HSM brand or 3rd party managed services. This is done using the HSM virtual partition and high availability features. When the customer subscribes to the service, the provider will partition the HSM and provide all the relevant access to the customer. The provider does not have access to the keys stored in the HSM; only the customer can access them. All key management operations shall be done remotely by the customer using the dual control mechanism.

Strategies you can consider

1. Do you need HSM?

Technically, a PKI system can operate without needing an HSM. However, storing keys on the local PKI system hard disk is not very secure. It is subject to various attacks to steal the keys. Just note that once the PKI is set up without an HSM, you will need to tear down and rebuild the PKI if you want to use an HSM.

2. HSM FIPS level

The most common HSM FIPS levels are level 2 and level 3. There are limited brands on level 4. Level 4 provides the most secure assurance in terms of protection. However, you need to be aware that some product vendors position their product in different manners. For example, some vendors will position their cryptographic module as a higher FIPS level and other modules as a lower FIPS level. In addition, the higher the FIPS level, the more expensive the HSM.

3. Key permutation and backup

When choosing the permutation, you must take into consideration the number of persons required to hold the package.

Permutation	Number of packages to generate	Number of persons to assigned	Number of persons to restore
2 of 4	4	4	2
3 of 6	6	6	3
4 of 8	8	8	4

4. To HA or not HA

Depending on how mission-critical the PKI services are, you can consider setting up the HSM in a high availability (HA) setup. However, when choosing the HSM brand, you need to be aware of whether it supports "Software high availability" or "Hardware high availability."

5. HSM Operation

From an operational perspective, you must provide a clean environment for the HSM so as not to trigger tampering. In addition, you must plan out the battery replacement for any HSM that has been in operation for more than 5 years. If you have a requirement that an HSM loaded with keys cannot be sent back to the factory for battery replacement, you must have an HSM replacement strategy to ensure that it does not affect the operation of PKI.

6. Crypto Currency HSM

If you have a requirement to store Crypto keys securely, you can consider getting an HSM brand that has such features. With this, you can consolidate your HSM operation.

7. HSM as a Service

There is always a concern whether the keys are secure when the HSM is not hosted in-house. Therefore, when subscribing to HSM as a Service or PKI as a Service, you need to review the security controls provided by the provider and any certification obtained when the HSM is running on the cloud. In addition, you also need to set up in-house processes to manage the HSM keys.

Key Ceremony

Key Ceremony is a process to provide assurance that keys are generated, stored, and backed up securely. In the PKI setup, this will involve HSM and Key Custodian. During the key ceremony for key generation, if this is for the Certification Authority, this is done using the Certification Authority software interfacing with the HSM. At this stage, there will be a few persons present to witness the generation:

- Key Ceremony Master of Ceremony that will manage the entire key ceremony process.
- Certification Authority Operator or authorizer that will operate the Certification Authority software.
- HSM key operator that will operate the HSM. Before the key generation commences, the HSM key operator must show that the HSM is blank with no key present.
- Independent witness that is invited to witness the entire process and attest that the process is legitimate and secure.

The key ceremony shall be done in a secure area to ensure that nobody can tamper with the process and illegally inject any key into the HSM. Once everything is ready, the Certificate Authority Operator will then use the Certification Authority software to initiate the key generate inside the HSM. Once the generation is done, the HSM key operator will then check the HSM to ensure that the keys are indeed stored in the HSM. Once this is verified, the Key Ceremony MC will then get everyone to sign-off that the key generation is done.

After the key generation is done, the HSM backup package will have to be generated. In here, the smart card (or USB thumb drive) used to store the backup shall be prepared and labelled. When the package is ready, the Key Custodians shall be called into the secure area to perform the key backup. The HSM key operator shall perform the key backup into the number of packages required based on the permutation agreed. For example, if it is agreed to have *2 of 4* permutations, then four packages shall be generated and handed over to the respective key custodians. The Key Matrix is then generated for safe-keeping and reference.

Strategies you can consider

Firstly, you need to decide on the type of permutation. This is because the more permutations, the more people you need to hold the package. In addition, the people selection criteria must be taken into consideration. Normally, we will advise that the packages be distributed among the head of department. However, assuming we are using *2 of 4*, then 2 of the heads of departments will require to come back to perform the key ceremony to restore the HSM when needed. Therefore, the people selection must coincide with the company's business continuity management so that the relevant people are available when needed. (i.e., 2 of the key custodians went on holiday and won't be able to bring the package to restore the HSM)

The venue of the Key Ceremony must be taken into consideration when performing the key ceremony. Some brands of HSM require the key generation to be done in front of the HSM. If the HSMs are stored in a secure data centre, then the access and security of the data centre must be taken into consideration. Besides, most of the time, a data centre is not designed to have a large crowd where you have 10-20 people crowded around the HSM to perform the key ceremony. How do you ensure that this group of people does not poke around the racks? If you are using the brand that has remote access console, then you can consider hosting the key ceremony crowd in a secure meeting room.

Key Archival System (KAS)

Originally, when PKI was designed, there was no Key Archival System (KAS). However, due to operational and security needs, KAS was added to the PKI system. The PKI system is designed using the Asymmetric encryption system, where only the Private Key can be used to decrypt the data encrypted with the Public Key. What happens if the Private Key is lost or stolen? In such cases, all data cannot be decrypted, and therefore the data can be considered lost forever. To avoid this, users can request a new Private/Public Key pair, but their data that was encrypted previously will be lost forever. To prevent this scenario, when the Private/Public key pair is generated, a copy of the Private Key is sent to the KAS for archival. This ensures that if the Private Key is lost, the Private Key can be recovered from the KAS system. In some implementations, the Private Key is stored on a smart card, which can be subjected to wear and tear, and sometimes the Private Key is not compromised, but the smart card is faulty and renders the Private Key unusable. In such cases, the PKI operator can recover the archived Private Key and re-insert it into a new Smart Card so that the user can resume their tasks.

Another use case for key archival is key recovery for investigation purposes. Imagine a user who has PKI and uses it to encrypt all the data that they steal and exfiltrate the encrypted data out of the company. Even if the data is intercepted, there is no way to find out the content of the data unless the private key is obtained. In such cases, investigators must retrieve the archived private key of that user and use it to decrypt the data without the knowledge of the user. Due to the sensitivity of the matter, the user will not know that their keys are being recovered for investigation purposes.

In typical implementation of KAS, all the user's private keys are stored in the KAS database encrypted by the KAS Symmetrical Key. This KAS Symmetrical Key become the crown jewel as once this key is compromised all the user's private keys shall be compromised. As such the security around this KAS key is very important. Depending on the brand of KAS, there are a few security implementations. The most basic implementation is to store the KAS key inside the HSM. This is to ensure that the KAS key is protected against tempering. In addition, some products allow key rotation as well. For example, the KAS Key is changed every X number of days and the entire data is decrypted and re-encrypt with the new key. Also, the physical control of the KAS system is also important to minimise the risk of being compromised by unauthorised personal.

Strategies you can consider

To deploy KAS, there are two ways to consider. In the first use case, where there is a need to recover a private key for a faulty card, the private key can be archived at the Credential Management System (CMS) (see the next section). In the second use case, a dedicated KAS is required, which can be deployed in a secured room for investigation purposes.

During the design phase, it's essential to consider whether the KAS function is needed. In addition, some brands may not support the KAS function, and in some cases, the KAS function is integrated with the CA function. Also, if there is a need for CMS, then whether the archival should be done at the CMS or the KAS, has to be taken into consideration.

For production and sensitive deployment, we would recommend having a dedicated HSM solely for storing the KAS Key and with proper Physical Controls being deployed to ensure that all the user's archived private keys are secured.

Some of our customers decided not to deploy a KAS system as there will be a lot of cost involved in securing the KAS system. Therefore, after evaluating the risk of data being lost forever vs the cost of protecting the KAS, they decided to forego the key archival functions. This will create some issues with their own users as there is a risk of data lost when the private key is damage or lost.

Credential Management System (CMS)

The Credential Management System (CMS) was formerly known as the Card Management System and is sometimes labelled as Identity Manager in certain products. Originally, the CMS was created to facilitate easy management of smart card issuance. In a best practiced PKI system, one user would have up to three certificates: an authentication certificate, an encryption certificate, and a digital signing certificate. These certificates would be generated, signed, and inserted into the smart card. From the perspective of the CA, this user would have three certificates, while from the user's perspective, they would only have one smart card. The issue arises when different types of certificates need to be managed and bound to the user. The CMS is used to bind all the certificates to a user. By using a CMS system, the PKI operator can know which smart card is issued to which user and how many certificates that user has.

From the above description, one could guess that a CMS is a Registration Authority of a CA. In the day-to-day operation of the CMS, a user who wants certificates will approach the CMS operator, who will check and verify the identity of the user based on a pre-defined process. Once the user's identity is confirmed, the CMS operator will use the CMS to generate key pairs and a certificate request. The CMS will then send the request to the CA for signing. Once the CA signs the certificate request, all of this information is injected into the smart card. If the user leaves the organization or loses the card, the CMS operator can use the system to revoke the user's certificates.

Subsequently, the Card Management System was renamed the Credential Management System as the CMS system was expanded to manage other forms of credentials like YubiKey, TPM Chip, Physical Access System, or any system that requires credential management.

Manufacturing Key Exchange

Some brands of CMS have a feature that only allows approved cards from manufacturers to be used to issue to users. This is accomplished by having a shared key between the card manufacturer and the customer's CMS. To set this up, there is a need to have a secure key exchange process to ensure that the shared key is securely generated and loaded into the Customer's CMS HSM via the Key Ceremony process. Once the shared key is loaded onto the CMS HSM, during card personalization, the CMS will check the card to see whether the pre-shared key exists in the card. If the pre-shared key is different, then the card will be rejected. This is to ensure that only the correct batch of cards from the approved manufacturer can be used. If the pre-shared key is the same, then the CMS will replace the pre-shared key on the smart card with the CMS-generated key and begin performing key generation and injecting certificates into the smart card. Once the smart card manufacturer key is swapped with the CMS-generated key, the smart card can only be managed by the CMS that swapped the key. No other CMS can be used. This is to ensure that user cannot bring the smart card to another CMS to manipulate the smart card content.

Credential Life-cycle Management

The following show the life cycle of credential being managed by the CMS:

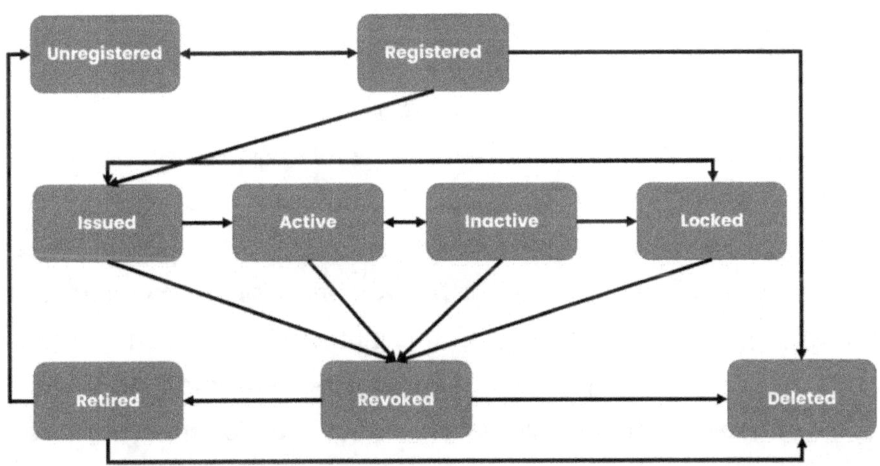

Figure 12 - Credential Life-cycle Management

Unregistered

When a credential has not been registered with CMS, it is flagged as unregistered. If physical token is used, CMS will read the token serial number to see whether it exist in the database. If it doesn't exist, then it is flagged as **Unregistered**.

Registered

Once a physical token is recognised, it is flagged as Registered. In this stage, the physical token manufacturing key is recognised and swapped out with a CMS-generated key. After the key is swapped, there is no way for the physical token to go back to the **Unregistered** stage. It can only go to the **Deleted** stage.

Issued

When a credential is issued, it will be labelled as **Issued**. In the PKI context, when a user is being issued with the appropriate certificates, it will be flagged as issued. Therefore, in some cases, when a user is being issued with Authentication, Decryption and Digital Signature certificates and this information is inserted into a smart card, the smart card is then labelled as **Issued**. The smart card will move on to the **Active** stage once the credential PIN is set. A credential can move to **Revoked** stage when the credential is being revoked.

Active

Most of the credentials will be in Active stage when it is actively in used and it can move to **Inactive** stage when being activated.

Inactive

Inactive stage is used when you want to temporary suspend the credentials. For example, someone misplace his/her token and being given a time to find the token. It can move to **Revoked** stage upon activation.

Locked

The credential can move to **Locked** stage when the PIN is blocked. For example, too many attempts on the smart card and hence being locked. In this stage, the CMS is needed to reset the PIN to move it back to **Issued** stage. Alternatively, the credential can be revoked, and it will move to **Revoked** stage.

Revoked

In this stage, all credentials are being revoked. In PKI case, the CRL will be updated with the revoked certificates. From here, the token can be set for deleted or recycle for new issuance.

Retired

At this stage, the credential or token is being prepared to be recycled for reused. However, the token can be permanently retired when it is moved to the **Deleted** stage.

Deleted

At normal operation, only credentials that are reported as damage, lost or stolen shall be in the **Deleted** stage. This will mean that the token cannot be used anymore.

Strategies you can consider

You need to consider whether you need a CMS or not. Without a CMS, you can already issue certificates to users with a Registration Authority. Some customers use an Excel file to track which certificates are issued to which user. This is manageable if the user base is small, but if it's large, using Excel will be difficult. By using a CMS, you eliminate errors and can use it to track certificates and security tokens (e.g., smart cards, YubiKeys, physical access, etc.) issued to users.

In some deployments, there is a segregation between the PKI Operator and CMS Operator. The PKI Operator's function is solely for certificate management (e.g., creation of certificate templates), while the CMS's sole function is to perform credential management for users. In this case, a CMS is needed by policy design.

A CMS has the key swapping function to ensure that only legitimate cards from approved manufacturers can be used. So, you need to decide whether you need this function. The risk of not having this function is that the CMS Operator can bring any smart card and use it. So, if your company issues security tokens to users, then this feature is highly recommended.

Certificate Distribution System (CDS)

A Certificate Distribution System (CDS) is a system where the Certification Authority publish all the certificates and certificate revocation list (CRL) where the applications can consume the information:

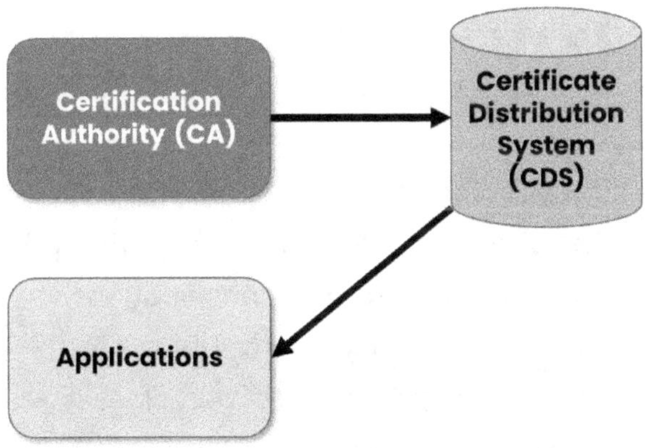

Figure 13- Certificate Distribution System

When a user certificate request is signed by the Certification Authority, the certificate is then published on the CDS. When a user certificate is revoked, it is published as a Certificate Revocation List (CRL) to the CDS. Therefore, applications must query the CDS periodically to check the status of the certificate when presented by the user.

Traditionally, the CDS is based on the X.500 directory or Lightweight Directory Access Protocol (LDAP). Due to the progression of technology, there are now many non-LDAP systems that can support LDAP interface. For example, Active Directory and its standalone version of ADLDS can support LDAP by default.

PKI certificate is based on the X.509 standard, which part of the X.500 series of standard. The X.500 consists of the following standards:

- X.500 - The Directory: overview of concepts, models and services
- X.501 – The Directory: Models
- X.509 – The Directory: Public Key and attribute certificate frameworks
- X.511 – The Directory: Abstract Service Definition
- X.518 – The Directory: Procedures for distributed operation
- X.519 – The Directory: Protocol specifications
- X.520 – The Directory: Selected attribute types
- X.521 – The Directory: Selected object classes
- X.525 – The Directory: Replication
- X.530 – The Directory: Use of systems management for administration of the Directory

The X.511 also defined the Directory Access Protocol (DAP) from which the LDAP protocol was adopted. Originally, the DAP protocol required the OSI stack to function, which created issues for deployment over the Internet. Hence, LDAP was born. LDAP is an industry-standard application protocol for accessing and maintaining distributed directory information services over an Internet Protocol network. LDAP is defined in RFC 4511, and it uses the description language ASN.1 (Abstract Syntax Notation One), which is also used in PKI.

Overview of LDAP protocol

The LDAP protocol begins with performing a **Bind** to a LDAP server to authenticate. The authentication can be named or anonymous. If the **Bind** is named, it is mostly for performing addition, modification, or deletion operations. Anonymous **Bind** is usually used for search requests. After all the operations are performed, the session is ended with an **Unbind** request.

Directory structure

The CDS used in PKI must be in a tree structure due to the influence of the X.500 specification. The Directory holds **"objects of interest"** or simply **"objects"**. Each object (also known as an entry) belongs to an object class. The object class identifies a family of objects that share certain characteristics and one or more attributes of that object class. Objects in a Directory is not case sensitive. Therefore, **cn=John Doe** is the same as **CN=JOHN DOE**. See the illustration below:

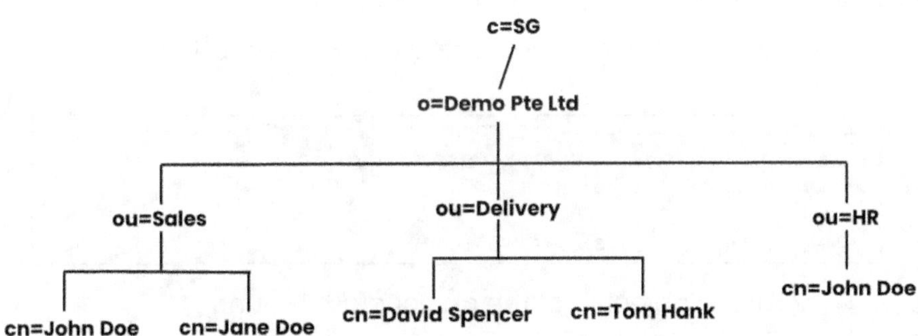

Figure 14- Sample LDAP structure

Terminologies used in directory:

- The structure is called Directory Information Tree or **DIT**
- o=Demo Pte Ltd is the **parent** of ou=Sales, ou=Delivery and ou=HR.
- ou=Sales, ou=Delivery and ou=HR are **children** of o=Demo Pte Ltd
- ou=Sales, ou=Delivery and ou=HR are **siblings**
- each entry is called an **object**. (e.g., c=SG is an object, cn=Tom Hank is an object)
- each **object** belongs to a certain class called object class. For example, c=SG belongs to the object class of **country**.
- Each object class has a pre-defined set of **attributes**, and this definition is called **Schema Definition** or **Schema** in short.

Object class and attribute schema definition

Object class is defined in the schema and an example of objectclass "country" as follow using the ASN.1 notation:

```
objectclass ( 2.5.6.2 NAME 'country' SUP top STRUCTURAL
  DESC 'A geographic entity described by a 2 letter ISO 3166
assigned country code'
  MUST c
  MAY ( searchGuide $ description ) )
```

- 2.5.6.2 is object id of the object class "country"
- "SUP top" means this objectclass "country" has a parent called "top"

- "STRUCTURAL" means the object class "country" inherit all the attributes from "top"; all "top" attributes shall be inherited and included under "country"
- "DESC" means a short description of the object class, this is purely for schema documentation purposes.
- "MUST" means that within the "country" object class, there is an attribute called "c" that is required to be filled.
- "MAY" means that within the "country" object class, there is an attribute called "description" that is optional to be filled.

Apart from object class definition, the schema also defined the characteristics of attributes. For example, the attribute called "c" from the "country" object class has the following definition:

```
cn: Country-Name
 ldapDisplayName: c
 attributeId: 2.5.4.6
 attributeSyntax: 2.5.5.12
```

- "attributeId" is the "c" object id
- "attributeSyntax" is the syntax allowed for "c" attribute. 2.5.5.12 means Unicode String is allowed.

In the nutshell, for each entry, the object class determines, what the entry is (person, configuration, machine etc), required attributes and optional attributes for the entry. In addition, each entry may have multiple object classes and hence has multiple required and optional attributes.

PKI Object class in LDAP Directory

The most used object class to store PKI user object in a LDAP directory is **inetOrgPerson**. **inetOrgPerson** inherit from

organizationalPerson, which inherit from **person** and finally **top** object classes. Therefore, **inetOrgPerson** will have all the attributes (required and optional) from **organizationalPerson, person** and **top** respectively. **inetOrgPerson** is defined in RFC 2798. **inetOrgPerson** has the following required and optional attributes:

Requires Attributes	CommonName (cn), objectClass, Surname (sn)
Optional Attributes	audio, businessCategory, carLicense, departmentNumber, description, destinationIndicator, displayName, employeeNumber, employeeType, facsimileTelephoneNumber, givenName, homePhone, homePostalAddress, initials, internationaliSDNNumber, jpegPhoto, l, labeledURI, mail, manager, mobile, o, ou, pager, photo, physicalDeliveryOfficeName, postOfficeBox, postalAddress, postalCode, preferredDeliveryMethod, preferredLanguage, registeredAddress, roomNumber, secretary, seeAlso, st, street, telephoneNumber, teletexTerminalIdentifier, telexNumber, title, uid, userCertificate, userPKCS12, userPassword, userSMIMECertificate, x121Address, x500UniqueIdentifier

inetOrgPerson is commonly used to store PKI User object is because it has most of the common attributes required to store a user information. However, if you need extra attributes that is not available (e.g. NRIC), you can also create your own object class and attributes and inherent **inetOrgPerson** object class. To do that, you need to apply for own OID from Internet Assigned Number Authority (IANA).

An example entry in LDIF format of John Doe under Sales will looks like this:

```
dn:cn=John Doe, ou=Sales, o=Demo Pte Ltd, c=sg
objectClass: top
objectClass: person
objectClass: organizationalPerson
objectClass: inetOrgPerson
uid:jdoe
cn: John Doe
sn: Doe
givenName: John
mail: john.doe@demo.com
userPassword: <hash value>
mobile: 91234567
userCertificate: <binary object>
userCertificate: <binary object>
userCertificate: <binary object>
```

- **cn** is short form for **commonName** and sn is short form for **surname.**
- **uid** stands for userID and it can be used to store user's login id
- **userPassword** is used to store user's hash password. Together with **uid**, an LDAP server can be used as LDAP based authentication system.
- User's certificates are stored in the userCertificate attribute, where one certificate per entry. So, if user has multiple

certificates, there will be multiple entries in the userCertificate attribute. In addition, the certificate is stored in the binary format. In PKI, once the user is issued with the certificate, the certificates will be published at user's entry in LDAP, under **userCertificate** attribute.

The Certification Authority certificate is also published to the CDS. Normally, it is published at the company's main entry, in this example, o=Demo Pte Ltd. The Certification Authority entry is created using the objectClass, **certificationAuthority** with the following information:

Requires Attributes	authorityRevocationList certificateRevocationList cACertificate
Optional Attributes	crossCertificatePair

- The required attribute, **authorityRevocationList** is used to store the revocation list of sub-CAs.
- The required attribute, **certificateRevocationList** is used to store the list of user's certificates that has been revoked. (See Certificate Revocation List for more details)
- The required attribute, **cACertificate** is used to store the Certification Authority certificate.
- The optional attribute, **crossCertificatePair** is used to store cross certification information.

Unique Key in the directory (DN)

In a directory architecture, a unique key to an entry in the directory is called Distinguished Name or DN in short.

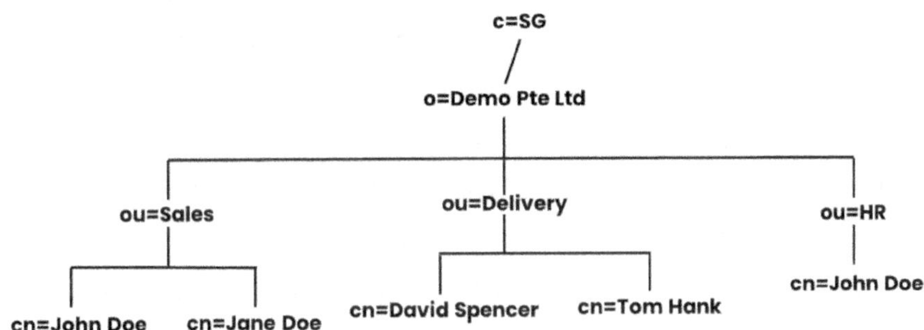

Using the above as an example, in the X.500 directory notation, John Doe entry under Sales is reference as: **@c=sg@o=Demo Pte Ltd@ou=Sales@cn=John Doe**. Using LDAP notation, John Doe entry is reference as: **cn=John Doe, ou=Sales, o=Demo Pte Ltd, c=sg**. If you try to create another **cn=John Doe** under Sales, an error will occurs as there is already a **cn=John Doe** exist. If you look at the example above, there are two John Doe:

Entry	Distinguished Name (DN)
John Doe in Sales:	**cn=John Doe, ou=Sales, o=Demo Pte Ltd, c=sg**
John Doe in HR:	**cn=John Doe, ou=HR, o=Demo Pte Ltd, c=sg**

Both are consider as unique entry as both have different DN.

Directory Operation

The Certificate Distribution System (CDS) is the most crucial component in the PKI system. It is primarily used by applications to check the status of certificates. Without a functioning CDS, applications will not be able to verify the certificate status and, as a result, deny user access. Therefore, CDS is typically deployed with a high availability design. As a result, the LDAP community has been looking towards directory replication and primary-secondary implementation. However, in the X.500 community, directory operation is built into the standard (defined in X.518), and products that support the X.500 standard can interoperate seamlessly. In contrast, there is no defined standard for interoperability between products in the LDAP community, making interoperation between different LDAP products challenging.

For LDAP deployment, there are a few models that can be used to ensure high availability:

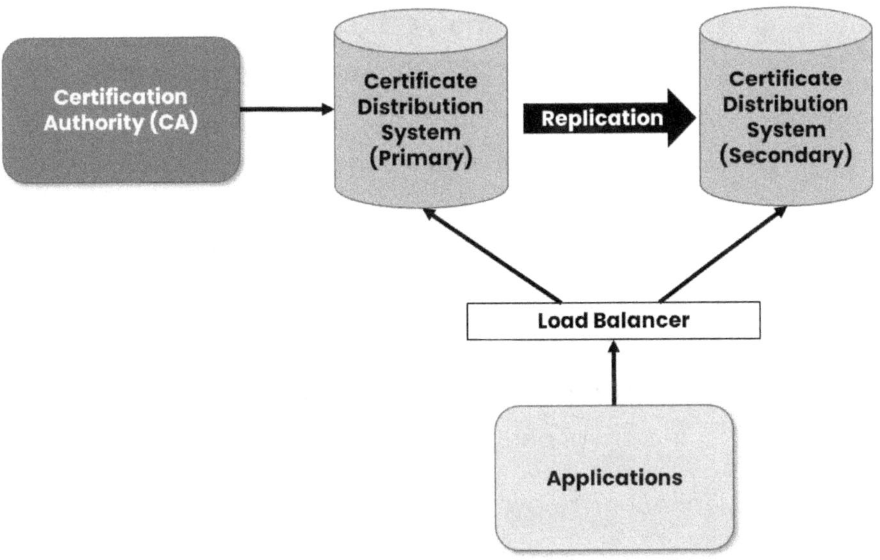

Figure 15- Simple High Availability

- CA publish the CRL and certificates to a Primary CDS.

- Primary CDS will perform replication to Secondary CDS. Note that most of the time, this can only works when both Primary and Secondary are from the same product vendor.

- The Applications query the CDS either going through the Hardware or Software Load Balancer or the Applications are designed to load balance internally between the two CDS. If any of the CDS is down, traffics can be routed to the CDS that is still available.

- Some points to consider:
  - The replication frequency vs the publication frequency. There is a window where the data is updated on Primary CDS but not available on Secondary CDS yet.

- o   The load on Primary CDS serving request from Applications and at the same time accepting update request from CA.
- o   Some load balancers can be configured based on load weightage. For example, 80% of the request will be forwarded to Secondary CDS and if the load on Secondary CDS is high, then some of the request shall be forwarded to the Primary CDS.
- o   Hardware Load Balancer vs Software Load Balancer in term of performance and cost.

Due to the limitations above, the above design can be enhanced as follow:

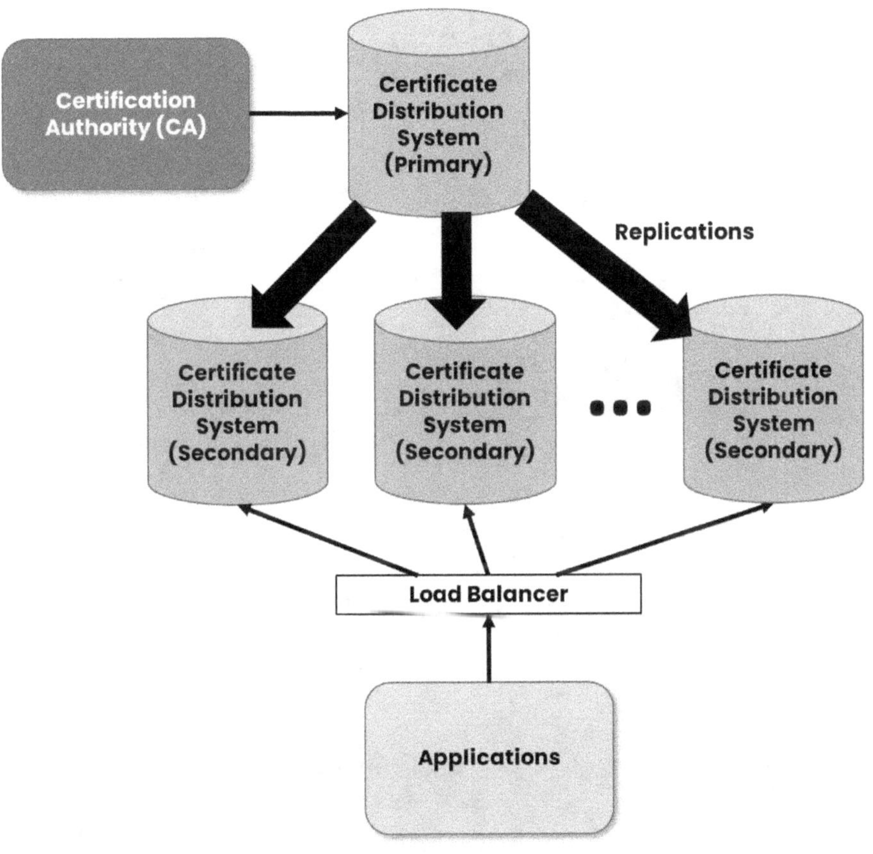

Figure 16- Multiple Secondary

- Similar to *Error! Reference source not found.*, except that P rimary CDS does not serve any Applications requests and solely for replication purposes.

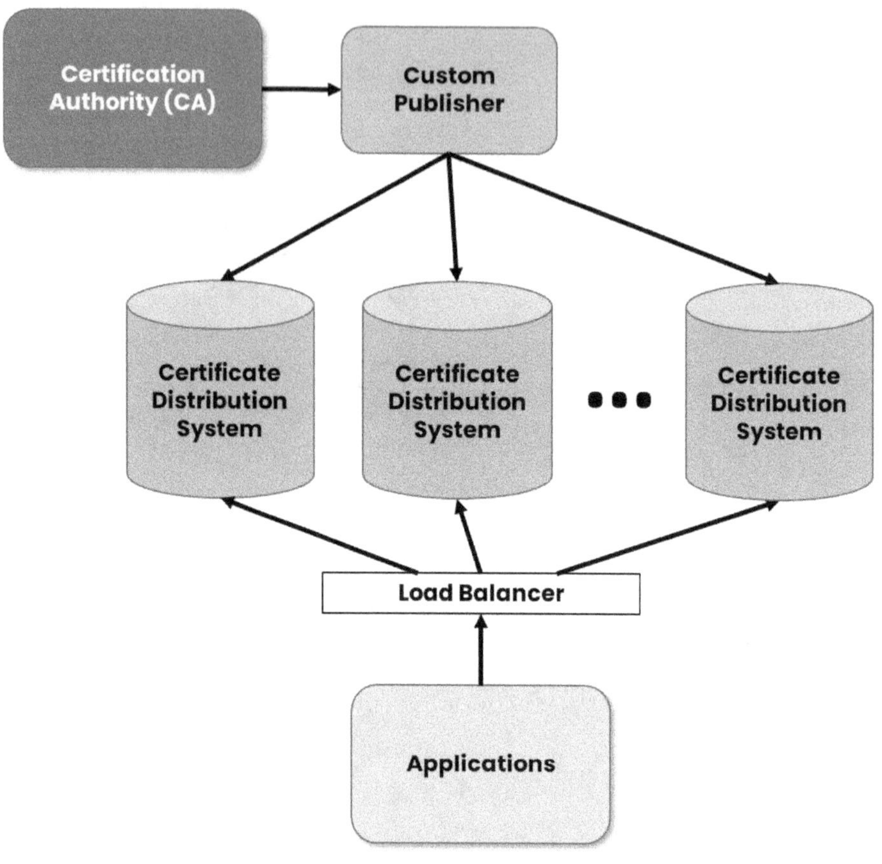

Figure 17- Custom Publisher

- In this design, a custom publisher is used to simultaneously publish the CRL and certificates to the CDS. This is to ensure that consistent data is being published on all the CDS. In addition, different CDS product vendors can be used as long as it supports LDAP protocol.

For more time sensitive and high availability type of deployment, the Global Server Load Balancing (GSLB) can be used.

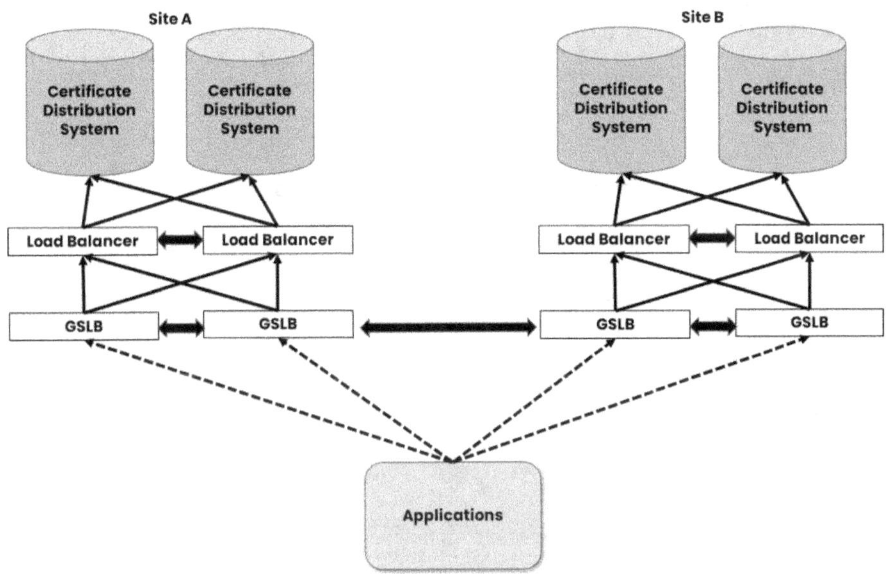

Figure 18- GSLB Deployment

- This design is to utilise the GSLB and LB technologies to provide high availability of the CDS to the applications.
- The CDS are deployed to minimum 2 sites for GSLB to work across 2 sites.
- GSLB pair will share the information across each pair

LDAP Data Interchange Format (LDIF)

LDAP Data Interchange Format (LDIF) is a standard plain text data interchange format for LDAP directory content. Most of the LDAP compliance server can support LDIF format. LDIF allows you to export the data out from one LDAP directory server to another, including Microsoft Active Directory or Microsoft ADLDS.

An example of LDIF to add an ou under o=Demo Pte Ltd, c=sg as follow:

```
Version: 1
dn:ou=Finance,o=Demo Pte Ltd,c=sg
changetype: add
objectClass: top
objectClass: organizationalUnit
ou=Finance
```

Data in LDIF format can be used to import entries into the LDAP server in bulk.

Certificate Revocation List (CRL)

Certificate Revocation List (CRL) is stored on the CDP for applications to query. The CRL stores all the user certificates that have been revoked. The Certification Authority periodically publishes the CRL to the CDP to ensure that all the revoked certificate information is up to date. The CRL is like a blacklist of certificates that a CA revokes prior to their assigned expiration dates. The CRL is time-stamped and signed by the Certification Authority. Since it is time-stamped, there is an expiry date to the CRL. The CRL is published to the CDP on a fixed interval, and this interval correlates with the expiry date of the CRL. If the CA is set up to publish the CRL on a weekly basis, then the CRL will have an expiry date of one week + one day. This is to ensure that if the publication fails, there is still a one-day window to remediate and republish the CRL. Just note that if the CRL is expired, the application will not be able to check the certificate status and hence should reject all requests. If PKI is used for system login, then if the CRL expires, all users will not be able to log in to the system.

CRL is also signed by the CA. When an application downloads the CRL, the application must ensure that the CRL is not tampered with, so it must verify the signature of the CRL using the CA's public key.

In a large high-turnover environment and after many years, the CRL can grow and become very big. This will pose a problem to the application that needs to download the CRL and search through the CRL to see whether the certificate presented is still valid while the user is still waiting for a response from the application. Some CA brands allow a subset of the CRL to be published at different points in the directory. For example, there will be a full CRL published on the organizational level, and there is also a sub-CRL for that specific department:

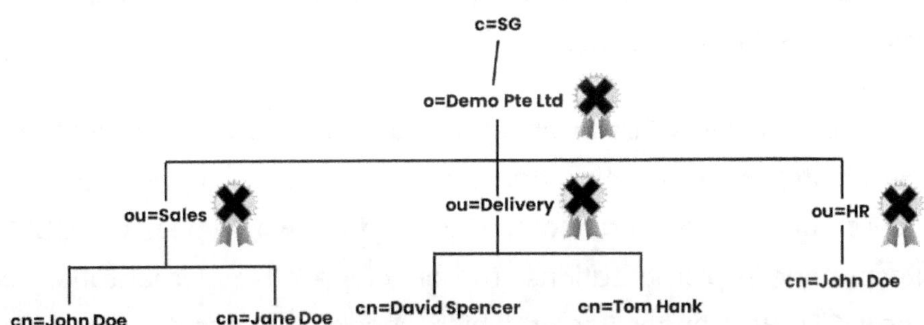

Figure 19- CRL Publication

In this example, the full CRL is published at o=Demo Pte Ltd. Then a subset of the CRL that is related to Sales is published to ou=Sales. Likewise, the same for ou=Delivery and ou=HR. The sub-CRL will only contain the revoked certificates pertaining to that OU. For this to work efficiently, the application must be aware of how to check the certificate presented, extract the department, and search the relevant department's CRL. (See the **Applications** section for more details.)

Online Certificate Status Protocol (OCSP)

CRLs are published to the CDP at fixed intervals. If a certificate is being revoked, then its revoke status is only published at the next publication interval. Assuming that a user certificate is being revoked after the current publication, the status will only be updated at the next publication. Therefore, the user certificate is still considered "valid" until the next publication because the CRL is not yet updated with the new revocation. However, ad-hoc publication can be initiated to update the CRL. Ad-hoc publication might impact PKI operations.

Instead of using CRLs to check the status of a user's presented certificate, an application can query an OCSP Responder on the user's presented certificate. There are two types of OCSP Responder implementations. The first type of implementation is the OCSP Responder Server, which checks with the CA on every OCSP query. The second type retrieves all the revoked certificates information from the CRL and pre-generates all the signed responses. The second type provides the fastest response to the certificate status request.

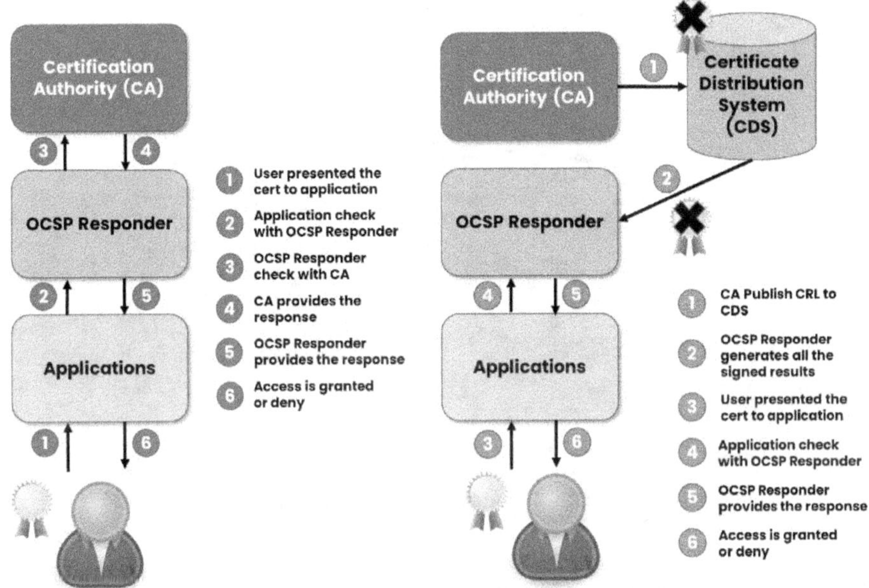

Figure 20- Type of OCSP deployment

For the second type of deployment, the OCSP Responder can be used to generate a revocation response of a particular user before the user is revoked by the CA. This is extremely useful if you are running some critical applications and want to revoke the user instantly before putting in a request to the RA Operator, or this could be an urgent revoke request due to fraud or compromise.

OCSP can also be used for distributed deployment to ensure a faster response to the Applications. This can be done by having multiple OCSP Repeaters deployed across the organization. A single OCSP Responder will replicate the information to all the OCSP Repeaters. In addition, there could be downstream OCSP Repeaters that receive replication from upstream OCSP Repeaters.

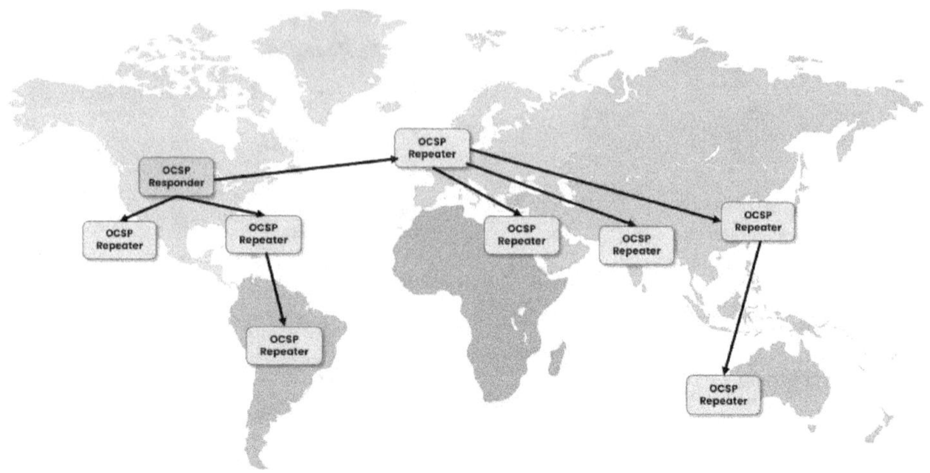

Figure 21- OCSP Responder/Repeater deployment

Strategies you can consider

Directory Structure

One aspect of PKI implementation that many overlook is the design of the directory structure. Once the PKI is established, it cannot be easily changed. For instance, if you begin with a country code of c=SG and later wish to change it, the entire PKI must be taken down and reconfigured. Moreover, the structure is embedded in the certificate, so altering the structure necessitates reissuing certificates. Consequently, some multinational corporations opt to use their domain name as the directory structure instead of c=<country code>. For instance, if a company's domain name is demo.com, then the directory structure could be:

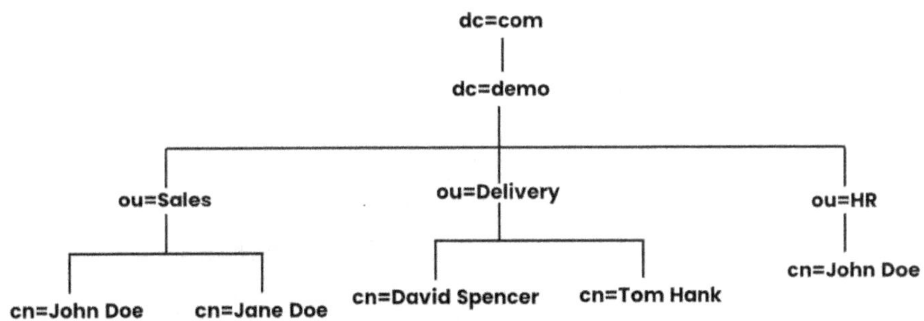

Figure 22- directory structure using dc

- dc is a short form for domainComponent

Apart from the directory structure, deciding on the "base" is also important. The "base" determines the primary ownership of the directory. For example, if the base is set to **o=Demo Pte Ltd**, then the CDS hosting **o=Demo Pte Ltd** will be the primary CDS server. For large MNCs, you can even design the CDS to host different branches of the directory. Note that the "base" will also impact how applications perform searches on the directory. More information is available under the **Applications** section.

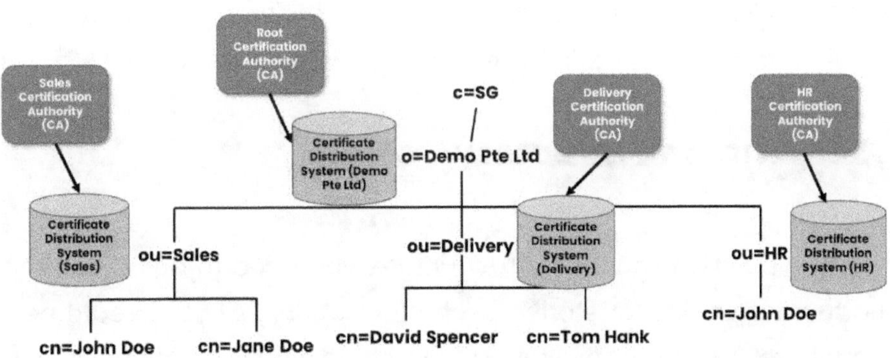

Figure 23- Multiple base deployment

- Based on *Error! Reference source not found.*, looking this in the Certification Authority perspective:

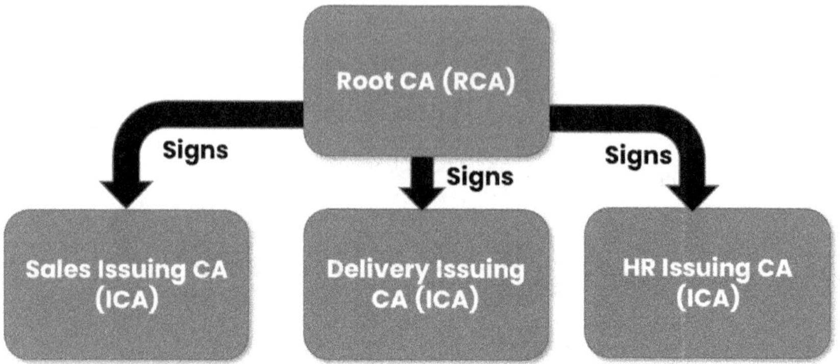

- The "base" for **CDS Demo Pte Ltd** is o=Demo Pte Ltd, c=sg
- The "base" for **CDS Sales** is ou=Sales,o=Demo Pte Ltd, c=sg. So, **CDS Sales** is the "master" for ou=Sales,o=Demo Pte Ltd.
- The "base" for **CDS Delivery** is ou=Delivery,o=Demo Pte Ltd, c=sg. So, **CDS Delivery** is the "master" for ou=Delivery,o=Demo Pte Ltd, c=sg
- The "base" for **CDS HR** is ou=HR, o=Demo Pte Ltd, c=sg. So, **CDS HR** is the "master" for ou=HR, o=Demo Pte Ltd, c=sg
- All the CDS are set to replicate their entries to each other so that they contain the entire organisation information.

Schema and Directory Design

Before building your PKI infrastructure, you need to decide on the attributes to use for storing user information. Will you create new attributes? If so, apply for OID numbers early. Additionally, you must decide on the object class to use for objects stored in the directory. You also need to consider your CDS. There are X.500-

based products, pure LDAP-based products, Microsoft Active Directory and Microsoft ADLDS. Whatever product you choose, consider its replication capabilities and high availability, whether you want to do a single primary and replicate to all the secondary or have a custom publisher to publish the information.

CRL, OCSP and Distribution Point

For CRL publication, decide on the CRL validity period and frequency of publication. You can consider deploying purely CDS for CRL publication, OCSP Responder only, or both. Depending on the product, you can reduce the size of CRL by having multiple distribution points.

For OCSP, there are different strategies to consider. You can use OCSP as a backup in case the CDS is not available. For large, distributed environments, you can consider having the OCSP Responder-Repeater type of deployment. Note that not all OCSP products have an OCSP Repeater architecture.

Certificate use cases and design

The standard and structure used for a certificate are defined in the X.509 specification. X.509 was initially issued together with the X.500 standards and later adopted by the Internet Engineering Task Force (IETF) PKIX working group as the PKI certificate standard. It is defined in RFC 5280 as *the Internet X.509 Public Key Infrastructure Certificate and Certificate Revocation List (CRL) Profile*. The current version of X.509 is version 3 and is widely used in the PKI community.

A X.509 certificate consists of the following fields: Version, Certificate Serial Number, Signature Algorithm Identifier, Issuer, Validity Period, Subject, Subject Public Key Information, Issuer Unique Identifier (Optional), Subject Unique Identifier (Optional), Extensions (Optional), and Certificate Authority's Digital Signature. During PKI setup, PKI templates are created to fill all the fields (except for the CA's Digital Signature) by the Registration Authority as PKCS #10 format and sent to the Certification Authority for signing. PKCS #10 defines the standard format for requesting signed X.509 certificates from the CA. Once the CA performs the validation, it then signs the certificate request, which becomes a usable certificate returned to the RA and published to CDS.

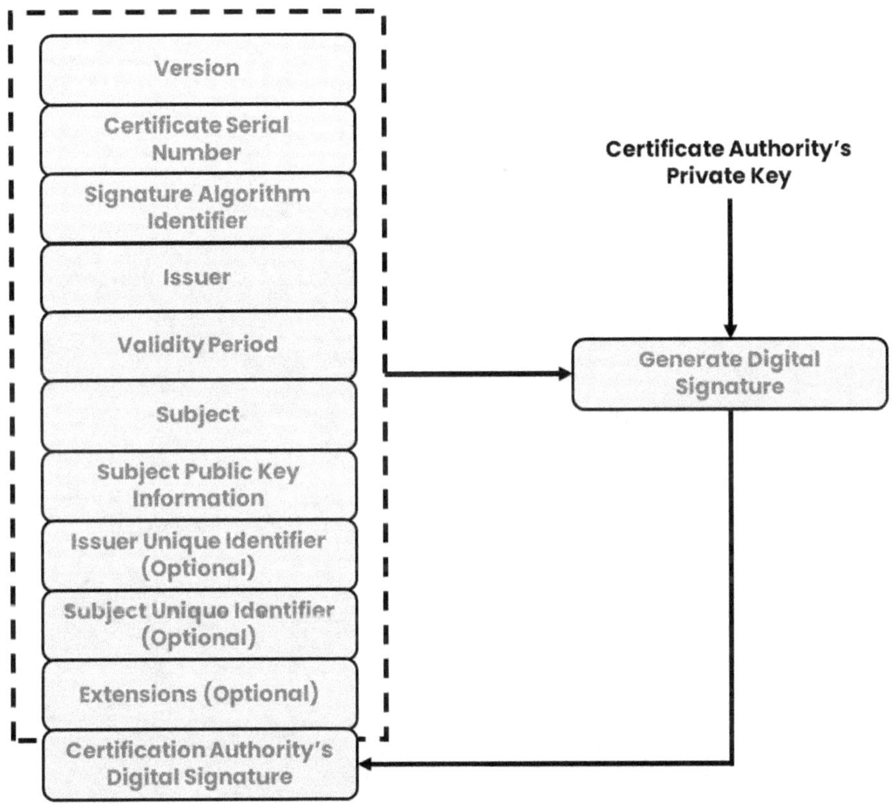

Figure 24- X.509 Certificate

The "Extensions" field allows customer to customise any specific information pertaining to the environment.

A sample Wikipedia certificate as follow:

```
Data:
    Version: 3 (0x2)
    Serial Number:
        10:e6:fc:62:b7:41:8a:d5:00:5e:45:b6
    Signature Algorithm: sha256WithRSAEncryption
    Issuer: C=BE, O=GlobalSign nv-sa, CN=GlobalSign Organization
Validation CA - SHA256 - G2
    Validity
```

```
                Not Before: Nov 21 08:00:00 2016 GMT
                Not After : Nov 22 07:59:59 2017 GMT
        Subject: C=US, ST=California, L=San Francisco, O=Wikimedia
Foundation, Inc., CN=*.wikipedia.org
        Subject Public Key Info:
            Public Key Algorithm: id-ecPublicKey
                Public-Key: (256 bit)
            pub:
                    00:c9:22:69:31:8a:d6:6c:ea:da:c3:7f:2c:ac:a5:
                    af:c0:02:ea:81:cb:65:b9:fd:0c:6d:46:5b:c9:1e:
                    9d:3b:ef
                ASN1 OID: prime256v1
                NIST CURVE: P-256
        X509v3 extensions:
            X509v3 Key Usage: critical
                Digital Signature, Key Agreement
            Authority Information Access:
                CA                          Issuers                   -
URI:http://secure.globalsign.com/cacert/gsorganizationvalsha2g2r1.crt
                OCSP                                                  -
URI:http://ocsp2.globalsign.com/gsorganizationvalsha2g2
            X509v3 Certificate Policies:
                Policy: 1.3.6.1.4.1.4146.1.20
                  CPS: https://www.globalsign.com/repository/
                Policy: 2.23.140.1.2.2
            X509v3 Basic Constraints:
                CA:FALSE
            X509v3 CRL Distribution Points:
                Full Name:

URI:http://crl.globalsign.com/gs/gsorganizationvalsha2g2.crl
            X509v3 Subject Alternative Name:
                DNS:*.wikipedia.org,           DNS:*.m.mediawiki.org,
DNS:*.m.wikibooks.org,  DNS:*.m.wikidata.org,  DNS:*.m.wikimedia.org,
DNS:*.m.wikimediafoundation.org,              DNS:*.m.wikinews.org,
DNS:*.m.wikipedia.org, DNS:*.m.wikiquote.org, DNS:*.m.wikisource.org,
DNS:*.m.wikiversity.org,                     DNS:*.m.wikivoyage.org,
DNS:*.m.wiktionary.org,                       DNS:*.mediawiki.org,
DNS:*.planet.wikimedia.org,  DNS:*.wikibooks.org,  DNS:*.wikidata.org,
DNS:*.wikimedia.org,                   DNS:*.wikimediafoundation.org,
DNS:*.wikinews.org,     DNS:*.wikiquote.org,     DNS:*.wikisource.org,
DNS:*.wikiversity.org,  DNS:*.wikivoyage.org,  DNS:*.wiktionary.org,
DNS:*.wmfusercontent.org,                  DNS:*.zero.wikipedia.org,
DNS:mediawiki.org,  DNS:w.wiki,  DNS:wikibooks.org,  DNS:wikidata.org,
DNS:wikimedia.org,    DNS:wikimediafoundation.org,    DNS:wikinews.org,
DNS:wikiquote.org,      DNS:wikisource.org,      DNS:wikiversity.org,
DNS:wikivoyage.org,    DNS:wiktionary.org,    DNS:wmfusercontent.org,
DNS:wikipedia.org
            X509v3 Extended Key Usage:
```

```
                    TLS   Web   Server   Authentication,   TLS   Web   Client
Authentication
          X509v3 Subject Key Identifier:

28:2A:26:2A:57:8B:3B:CE:B4:D6:AB:54:EF:D7:38:21:2C:49:5C:36
          X509v3 Authority Key Identifier:

keyid:96:DE:61:F1:BD:1C:16:29:53:1C:C0:CC:7D:3B:83:00:40:E6:1A:7C
     Signature Algorithm: sha256WithRSAEncryption
          8b:c3:ed:d1:9d:39:6f:af:40:72:bd:1e:18:5e:30:54:23:35:
```

- **Version**: the current version is 3.

- **Serial Number**: Unique certificate serial number

- **Signature Algorithm**: The algorithm used for signing

- **Issuer**: The distinguished Name of the Certification Authority

- **Validity**: Certificate validity, set as "Not Before" and "Not After"

- **Subject**: the distinguished Name (DN) of the certificate. This could be user's DN or domain name if this is SSL certificate.

- **Subject Public Key Info**: The public Key information of the subject. If this is a user, then it is the Public Key information of the user's certificate.

- **X509v3 extensions**: extended attributes for more refined usage. Some commonly used attributes are:

  - **X509v3 Key Usage:** this outlined the purpose of key. Applications should check for this to ensure that the appropriate key is used for the intended purposes. The Key Usage that was defined in RFC 5280:

Key usage value (RFC 5280)	Description
DigitalSignature	The key is used to verify digital

	signatures other than signatures on certificates and CRLs, for those used in entity authentication service, data origin authentication service and/or an integrity service.
nonRepudiation	The key is used to verify digital signatures other than signatures on certificates and CRLs, for those used in non-repudiation service that protects against the signing entity falsely denying action.
keyEncipherment	The key is used for encryption of private or secret key, i.e. for key transport.
dataEncipherment	The key is used for direct encryption of raw user data.
keyAgreement	This key is used for key management.
keyCertSign	This key is used for verifying signatures on public key certificates. This is normally used by the Certification Authority.
cRLSign	This key is used to verify signature on CRL.
encipherOnly	This key is used in conjunction with **keyAgreement.** During key exchange, the **encipherOnly** key is used for encryption.

decipherOnly	This key is used in conjunction with **keyAgreement.** During key exchange, the **decipherOnly** key is used for decryption.

- o **Authority Information Access:** this is normally a URL pointing to a CDS where the Certification Authority certificate is published.

- o **X509v3 Certificate Policies:** an URL pointing to where the Certificate Policy and Certificate Practice Statement is published. (See ***Certificate Policy and Certificate Practice Statement*** for more details)

- o **X509v3 CRL Distribution Points:** an URL that points to where the CRL is stored. If the URL prefix is http:// or https:// then the CRL can be accessed using http: or https: protocol. If the URL prefix is LDAP:// then the Applications need to connect to the LDAP server via the LDAP protocol.

- o **X509v3 Subject Alternative Name:** this field is mainly used in SSL certificate where multiple domains can be used for one SSL certificate.

Strategies you can consider

The first step is to consolidate all the certificate use cases, decide on the key usage for those use cases, and then create the relevant certificate templates. Some companies might not want to expose their internal PKI deployment and, therefore, might not be comfortable having **Authority Information Access** and **X509v3 CRL Distribution Points** filled up with values. Also, once the value is set on the certificate, it cannot be changed. The certificate must be revoked and reissued.

Applications

Applications have three main use cases with regards to PKI: authentication, non-repudiation, and encryption. The following is the high-level flow when an application receives and processes the certificate presented:

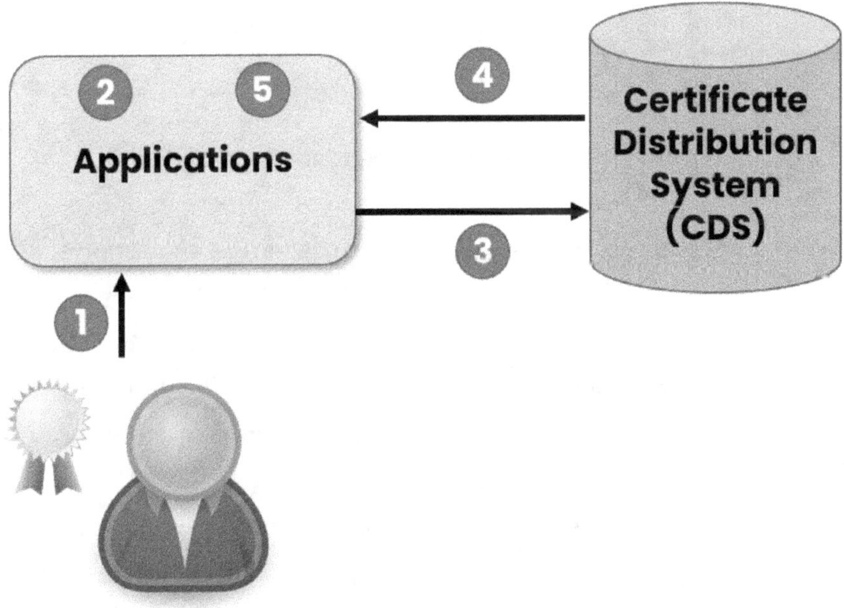

Figure 25- High level certificate processing

- **1** User presented the certificate to the application.

- **2** Application performs a basic certificate verification, which includes:
    - o Check the **Validity** to ensure that the certificate is valid.

- o The intended operation matches the key usage; for example, data encryption requires the key usage to be **dataEncipherment**.

- **(3)(4)** Query and retrieve from the CDS:
  - o the latest Certificate Revocation List (CRL).
  - o The Certification Authority Certificate. This can be optional as Applications can have a Certificate Store to hold all the trusted CA certificates.
  - o User certificate (optional)

- **(5)** Application to perform the following validation:
  - o Validate the CA certificate and its chain of trust. This includes checking of the Authority Revocation List (ARL) to ensure that the CA certificate is not revoked.
  - o Check the CRL signature using the validated CA certificate.
  - o Validate the presented certificate to ensure that the signature is valid.
  - o Once all check is ok, then the intended operation can be executed.

Validate the CA Certificate and its chain of trust.

Applications must perform CA Certificate chain of trust verification. For example, if there is **Root CA** that is self-signed, the **Root CA** will sign the **Intermediate CA** and in turn sign the **Issuing CA**.

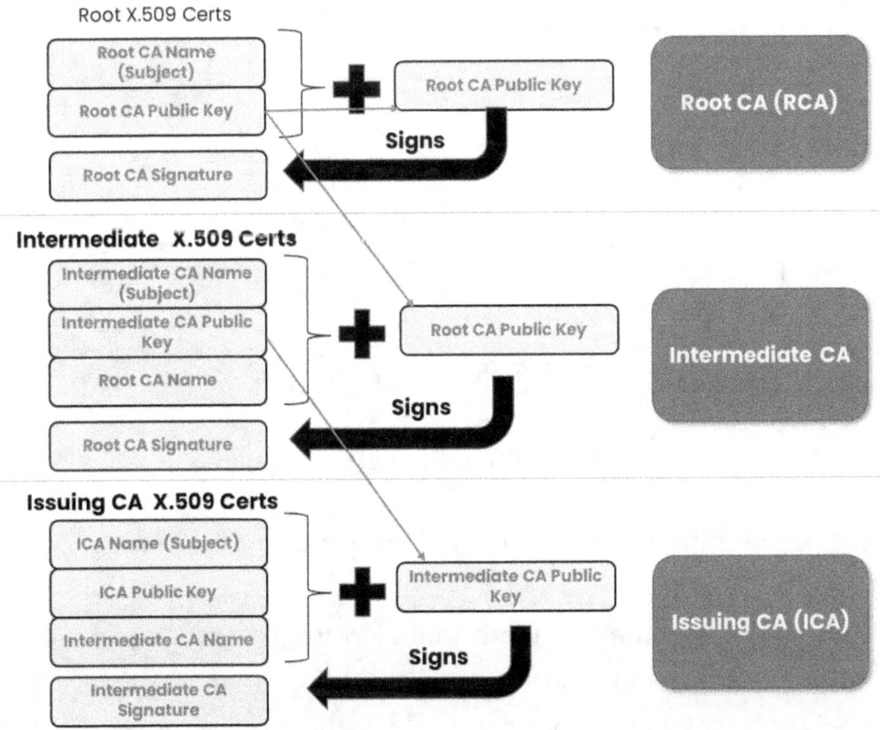

Figure 26- Certificate chain of signing

During the chain of trust verification:

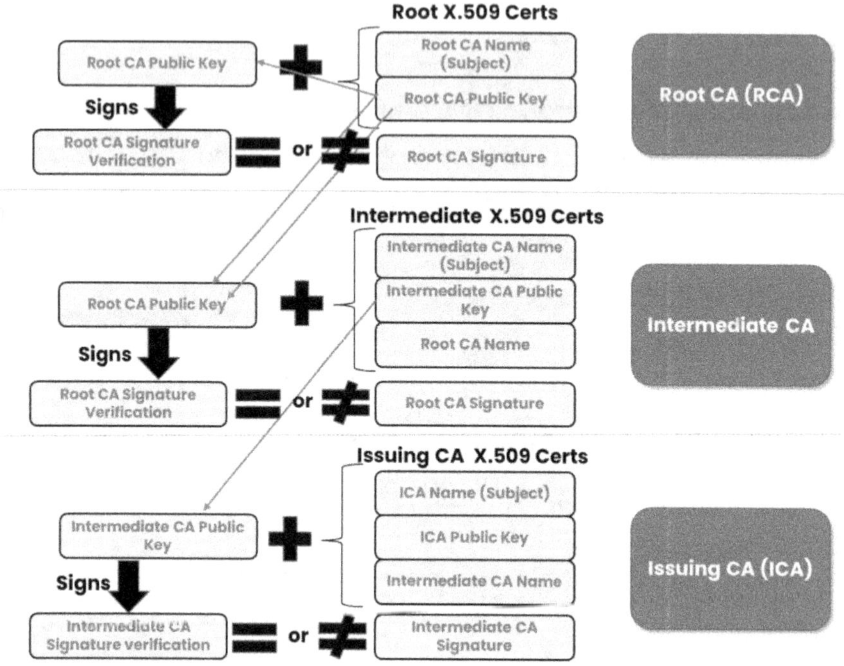

Figure 27- Chain of trust verification

- Starting from Issuing CA, check that the Issuing CA dates are valid.
- Retrieve the CA name that sign the Issuing CA certificate (Intermediate CA)
- Retrieve the Intermediate CA certificate from CDS, retrieve the Authority Revocation List (ARL), check that the issuing CA and Intermediate CA are not in the ARL.
- Check that both issuing CA and Intermediate CA dates are valid.

- Retrieve the Intermediate CA's Public Key and use it to verify that the Intermediate CA Signature at the Issuing CA Certificate is valid.
- Retrieve the Root CA Name from Intermediate CA Certificate.
- Retrieve the Root CA certificate from CDS, check that the Root CA are not in the ARL.
- Check that the Root CA certificate dates are valid.
- Retrieve the Root CA's Public Key and use it to verify that the Root CA Signature at the Intermediate CA Certificate is valid.
- Use the Root CA's Public Key and use it to verify that the Root CA Signature at the Root CA Certificate is valid.

Searching the CDS using LDAP protocol

As you can see from now, Applications will need to perform a lot of LDAP Search to the CDS. On windows, you can download the **ldapsearch.exe** command line to perform the LDAP Search on any CDS.

```
ldapsearch -x -b <search_base> -H <ldap_host>
<search filter>
```

- -x without any login id and password will login to the LDAP Server as anonymous.
- -b is telling the LDAP Server where to search from
- -H <ldap_host> is the LDAP Server IP or server name

- <search filter> is the search filter to return. If you put "*", it will return all entries. Note that some LDAP Server will limit the number of entries return for a LDAP Search, for example first 200 entries.

Using the following directory structure as an example:

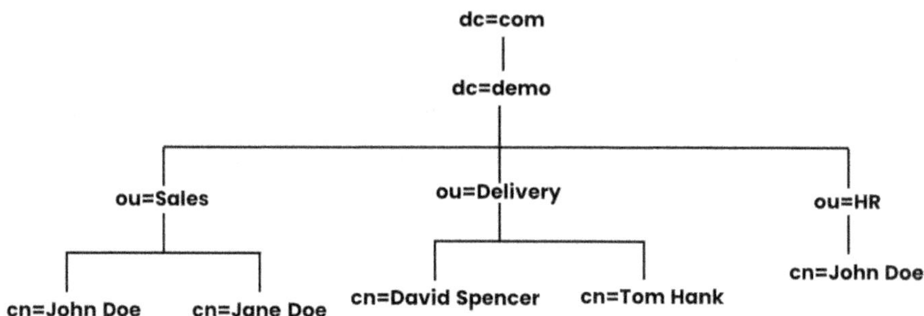


1. ```
   Ldapsearch -b dc=demo,dc=com -H ldap.demo.com
   "(cn=*)"
   ```
   a. This will return entries that has the attributes "cn="; in the example above, it will return all entries.
2. ```
   Ldapsearch -b dc=demo,dc=com -H ldap.demo.com
   cn=John Doe
   ```
   a. This will return 2 entries; ***cn=John Doe, ou=Sales, dc=demo, dc=com*** and ***cn=John Doe, ou=HR, dc=demo, dc=com.***
3. ```
   Ldapsearch -b ou=Sales, dc=demo, dc=com -H
   ldap.demo.com cn=John Doe
   ```
   a. This will return 1 entry; ***cn=John Doe, ou=Sales, dc=demo, dc=com***
4. ```
   Ldapsearch -b cn=John Doe, ou=Sales, dc=demo,
   dc=com -H ldap.demo.com cn=John Doe
   ```
   a. This will return 1 entry; ***cn=John Doe, ou=Sales, dc=demo, dc=com***

As you can see from above, setting the base is very important to narrow down the search. In addition, the base can be constructed from the X.509 certificate being presented (from the Subject field). For example, John Doe at Sales will have the following LDAP distinguishedName: ***cn=John Doe, ou=Sales, dc=demo, dc=com***. This will be embedded in John Doe's X.509 certificate as the "**Subject**" field. Applications can retrieve this from the certificate presented and search the CDS. This will provide a more efficient and faster way to search the LDAP Directory.

So far, the most commonly search done by Applications are:

```
Ldapsearch -b dc=demo,dc=com -H
ldap.demo.com "(objectClass=*)"
```

This will return all the entries in the LDAP Server (up to the return limit). The Application will then have to parse the return results one by one to search for the entry that is needed. It will be very efficient if the direct entry search (example #4) is used.

Strategies you can consider

If an LDAP server is used for authentication and access control, the speed of the application processing the search becomes crucial. Therefore, it is important that the application can minimize the search and process the return results quickly. As such, it is important that the application is optimized so that processing can be done quickly.

Some applications will cache some of the actions. For example, the CA chain verification can be done once a day, and the result can be cached in the application. The application can then only perform individual certificate verification. Likewise, the Certificate Revocation List and Authority Revocation List verifications must coincide with the frequency of publication so that verification can be cached. However, if the application is sensitive, it is better to perform a full verification every time a certificate is presented.

Certificate Policy & Certificate Practice Statement

The Certificate Policy (CP) and Certificate Practice Statement (CPS) is defined in the IETF RFC 3647. The CP and CPS are normally used in commercial PKI as both has legal implications. As per RFC 3647:

> *A certificate policy (CP) is "a named set of rules that indicates the applicability of a certificate to a particular community and/or class of applications with common security requirements." A CP may be used by a relying party to help in deciding whether a certificate, and the binding therein, are sufficiently trustworthy and otherwise appropriate for a particular application.*

On the other hand, a CPS is a statement of the practices which a certification authority employs in issuing certificates.

Together, both documents shall provide assurance from the Certification Authority on the level of security it can provide. In most cases, liability clauses are included in the CP and CPS. For example, a Certification Authority can offer different classes of certificates with different sets of pricing. A class "A" certificate might cost "XX" amount with a liability of "YY" amount. A class "B" certificate might cost "X" amount with a liability of "Y" amount. A class "A" certificate might have to go through a more stringent registration process as it is more expensive and also higher liability. This means that if a class "A" certificate is compromised, the customer can claim up to "YY" amount from the Certification Authority. Therefore, CP and CPS are normally drafted by the legal department.

Strategies you can consider

CP and CPS are normally used in commercial PKI. For in-house PKI implementation, it is best to have a PKI policy defined, organization wide. This is to ensure that everyone in the organization will adhere to the policy. Some of the areas that you need to take note of in your policy includes:

- Cryptography embargo statement: This is to ensure that your organization did not purchase any products that are produced by certain countries that are being barred.
- Cryptography algorithm statement: This is to ensure that your organization does not use any algorithm that is not secure (e.g., DES or triple-DES). In addition, you might want to state the minimum requirement for certain types of usage (e.g., key length of RSA-3072 is to be used for Certification Authority Public/Private Key Pair).
- Usage of Hardware Security Module, Key Ceremony requirement, and Key Custodian requirement.
- Rough Certification Authority requirement: Normally, rough CA is not allowed in the organization as rough CA might not follow the pre-defined security controls. In addition, there is a need to perform regular scans of the network to discover rough CA. Having a centralized CA will

ensure that all the trust is centralised in a single place for easy management and verification processes.

- Key Usage: For example, for what purpose, then what is the minimum key length requirement. This is to ensure that the system is protected appropriately.
- PKI Operation requirement: Who is the owner and who can operate the PKI? What are the staffing requirements? E.g., Outsource the PKI Operation or deploy on cloud?
- Key Management and key-rollover strategy of PKI system.
- Key Archival policy: Users need to understand what the potential use cases are for key archival. For example, if a user's keys can be retrieved for investigation purposes, it has to be stated clearly in the policy.
- PKI hardware/software certification requirements: For example, only FIPS 140-2 level 3 HSM can be used, etc.
- PKI usage in OT environments. See: **PKI – the Forgotten Child in IT, Star Child in OT**

Security Token and PKI

There are many security tokens in the market and sometimes we might misinterpret it as PKI security token. Security Token is used mainly to satisfy the 2FA requirement of "what you have" and together with Password (What you know), form the two factors of Authentication (2FA).

There are two types of Security Token. The first type is the physical token type. This is similar to the token that banks used to issue to the customer for them to access to the internet banking application. Normally, for this type of physical token, it must be issued by the relevant parties and not easily purchasable from the Internet. Some token will continuously be showing numbers on the screen and the number will periodically refresh at fixed interval. One prominent form of physical security token that is widely used is Smart Card, which will be covered in the next section.

The second type of security token is software based and normally installed on android or Apple smart phone. This software together with the smart phone form the "What you have" form factor of 2FA. Similar to the Physical Security Token, the software will generate some random number to be used for authentication purposes. There is also software smart card that can be installed on smart phone to be used like a physical smart card.

Physical Smart Card

A physical smart card, which is also known as chip card or integrated circuit card (ICC) is typically a plastic credit card-sized card with an embedded integrated chip (IC). The IC plastic card was invented in the late 60's and become mainstreams in the 70's with the term Smart Card being commonly used.

There are a few types of Smart Card which most of us are familiar with. One of them is the Credit Card with a chip cleared shown on the front. This type of card is mainly used in the payment system and being defined in the Europay MasterCard Visa (EMV) standard. The driver for the EMV type of card to be used for payment is due to the fact that magnetic strip on the card is easily copied. In the late 90's, there is a major push by the credit card company to move the payment system to chip-based so as to mitigate the risk of credit card information being stolen via the magnetic strip.

Another type of Smart Card is widely used in the mobile phone is called the SIM (Subscriber Identity Module or Subscriber Identification Module) Card intended to securely store the international mobile subscriber identity (IMSI) number and its related key, which are used to identify and authenticate subscribers on mobile telephony devices. SIM cards store network-specific information used to authenticate and identify subscribers on the network. The most important of these are the ICCID, IMSI, authentication key (Ki), local area identity (LAI) and operator-specific emergency number. The SIM also stores other carrier-specific data such as the SMSC (Short Message Service Centre) number, service provider name (SPN), service dialling numbers

(SDN), advice-of-charge parameters and value-added service (VAS) applications.

The smart card that is commonly used in PKI is also known as Java Card. The Java Card is a software technology that allows Java-based application, also known as Applet, to be run securely on the smart card. Java Card gives the flexibility to develop your own Java based specific application to be run on the smart card. The first Java Card was introduced in 1996 by Schlumberger's card division which later merged with Gemplus to form Gemalto. Java Card products are based on the specifications by Sun Microsystems (later a subsidiary of Oracle Corporation). Many Java card products also rely on the Global Platform specifications for the secure management of applications on the card (download, installation, personalization, deletion).

Smart Card normally comes in the form of plastic card with design printed on the plastic part. The material for the card could be made of PET or PVC plastic. PET, or polyethylene terephthalate plastics is one the most widely used plastics for thermoforming. The material is moulded into the designated shape, and then dried for increased resistance. The plastic is used to produce food containers, beverage bottles, synthetic fibres and more. PET is the most common plastic for thermoforming packaging designs because of its high-strength barrier that can resist outside tampering or other elements.

PVC plastic, or polyvinyl chloride, is a rigid plastic designed to withstand harsh impacts and extreme temperatures. The material is most used when creating cables, roofing materials, commercial signage, flooring, faux leather clothing, pipes, hoses and more. PVC plastic is created through suspension polymerization to produce a hard, rigid structure.

PET Smart Card is mainly used if the card is exposed to harsh environments with high UV exposure. PET Smart Card is more expensive than a PVC Smart Card.

Type of Java card

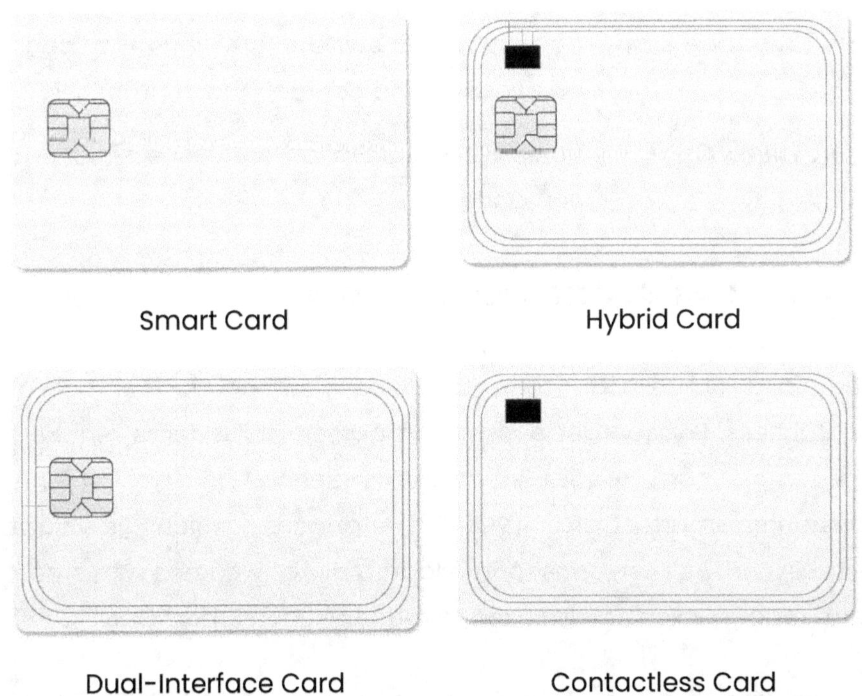

Smart Card

Hybrid Card

Dual-Interface Card

Contactless Card

Type of Java Card	Characteristics
Smart Card	Single chip only card. Information can only be access via contact.
Hybrid Smart Card	2 separate chips, one for contact and another for contactless. Both chips store different information. Normally used for logical security via contact (PKI) and physical security via contactless (door access).
Dual-Interface Card	1 chip with the same information that can be accessed via contact and contactless.
Contactless Card	1 chip with information only accessible via contactless.

Contact vs Contactless access

The Java Smart Card can be access either via contact or contactless. For contact access, a smart card reader is required. The smart card reader standard is defined in the Personal Computer/Smart Card (PC/SC) standard which is quite established. As such, most of the laptop already comes with smart card reader which can be used to read the Java Smart Card.

For contactless, the standard used is defined in ISO/IEC 14443 which communicate via radio at 13.56 MHz and have an operational range of up to 10 centimetres. ISO/IEC 14443 is the primary contactless smart card standard being used for transit, financial, and access control applications. It is also used in electronic passports. Just note that ISO/IEC 14443 is also used by Near Field Communication (NFC) which is common in smart phone.

Java Card Security

As of writing, the latest java card version is version 3.2, which was released on 30th Jan 2023, with support for TLS 1.3 protocol. Java Card technology was originally developed for the purpose of securing sensitive information stored on smart cards. Security is determined by various aspects of this technology:

Data encapsulation

Data is stored within the application, and Java Card applications are executed in an isolated environment (the Java Card VM), separate from the underlying operating system and hardware.

Applet firewall

Unlike other Java VMs, a Java Card VM usually manages several applications, each one controlling sensitive data. Different applications are therefore separated from each other by an applet firewall which restricts and checks access of data elements of one applet to another.

Cryptography

Commonly used symmetric key algorithms like DES, Triple DES, AES, and asymmetric key algorithms such as RSA, elliptic curve cryptography is supported as well as other cryptographic services like signing, key generation and key exchange.

Applet

The applet is a state machine which processes only incoming command requests and responds by sending data or response status words back to the interface device.

Certification

Like HSM, most of the commercial smart card manufacturers will send their smart cards for NIST FIPS certification. This is to provide security assurance of the cards. Therefore, there are smart cards that are FIPS 140-2 level 2 or 3 certified. In addition, some smart card manufacturers will brand their smart card as level 3 certified but upon checking, their level 3 certification is only for their crypto module and the overall certification can be only at level 2.

Smart Card Chip Components

Smart Card Chip is effectively a small computer with the approximately same computing power as the first IBM PC. The components of smart card chip components as follows:

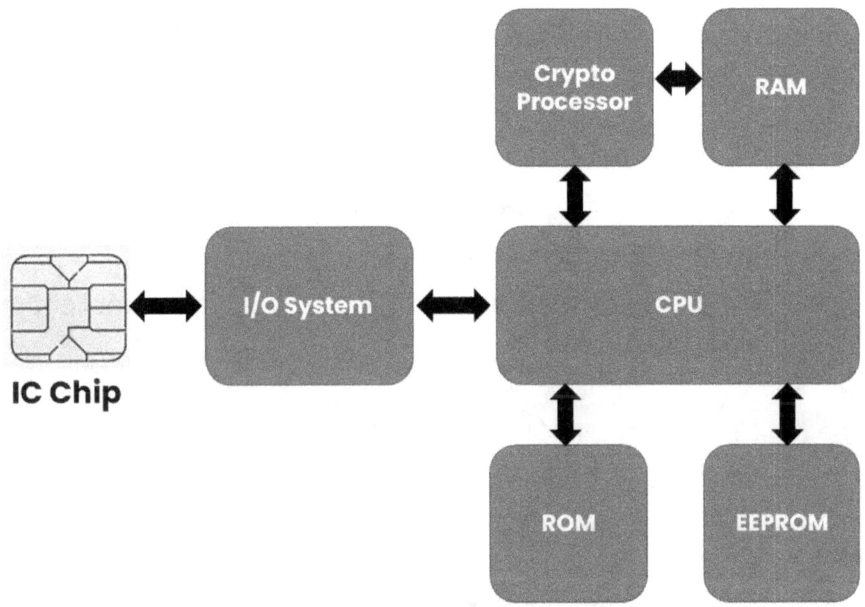

Figure 28 - Smart Card Chip Components

- IC Chip interface with the rest of the components via the **I/O System**.

- The **CPU** can range from 8-bit microprocessor to 32-bit microprocessors.

- The **Crypto Processor** is used specifically to perform crypto functions like Encryption using the user's private key which is stored in the EEPROM. In this way, the user's private key will never leave the card and all encryption function is done on the card itself.

- The **RAM** is the transient memory of the card and keeps the data only as long as the card is powered.

The information in the **ROM** is written during production. It contains the card operating system and sometimes, applet developed by the card manufacturer.

- The **EEPROM** is used for permanent storage of data. Even the card is unpowered, the data in EEPROM remain intake. Some smart cards allow storing of additional application code or applet.

The RAM, ROM and EEPROM come with various sizes depending on the manufacturer. It can range from a few hundred KB to a few MB.

Customer, when purchasing smart card from manufacturer, has the option to pre-load the applet onto the smart card ROM during production. Alternatively, the smart card can be shipped without the applet and customer will have to load their own applet using the Credential Management System (CMS) during card personalisation.

Communication with Smart Card

The native communication with smart card is via APDU (application protocol data unit) command defined in ISO/IEC 7814-4. It defined the command to send to smart card and the response packet received from smart card.

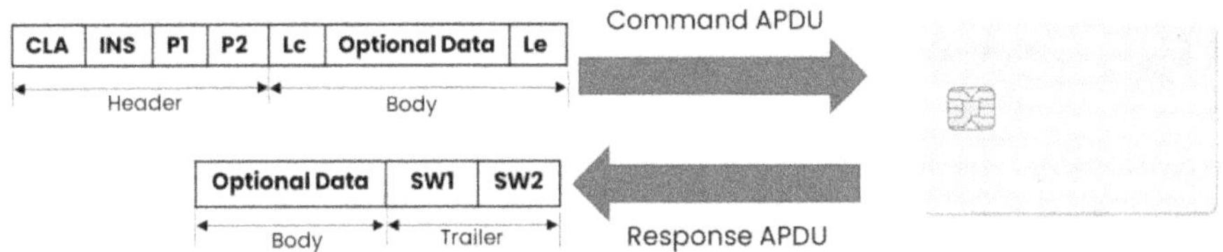

Figure 29 - communication with smart card

Because of this complexity in passing command and processing the response, most of the smart card manufacturer will provides software (**smart card middleware**) that will help to communicate with the smart card. Some of this middleware allows applications to be developed to interface with the smart card and this is normally done using the published standard API like PKCS #11 or Microsoft Crypto API.

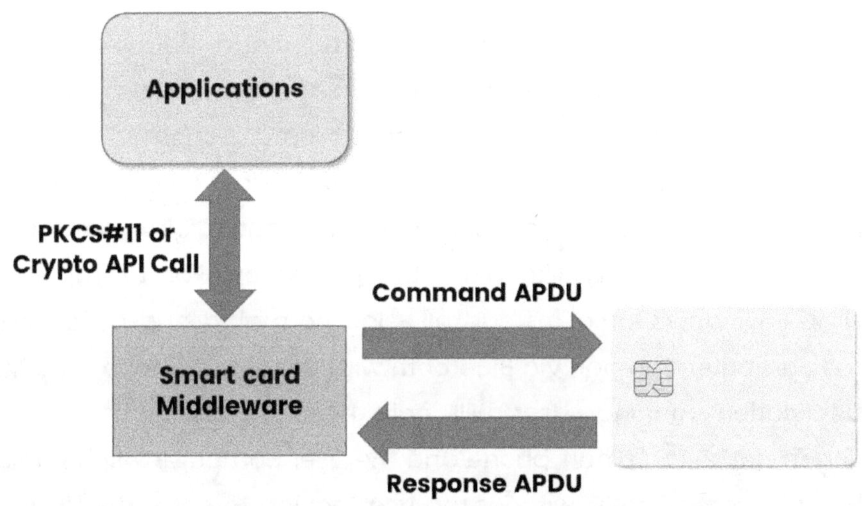

Figure 30 - Applications interface with smart card

USB Token

Apart from having IC Chip on a credit card size form, the smart card can be in USB Token form. This USB token with the same functionality as smart card, can be easily plugged into the USB port of the computer. This eliminates the needs of having Smart Card Reader.

However, when choosing the USB token brand, you need to be aware that not all USB Token can be used as PKI Smart Card as some USB Token only support FIDO/FIDO2 authentication, which is not a full implementation of PKI.

Virtual Smart Card

Due to advancing in technology in the smart phone area in particular the usage of secure chip on the smart phone, smart phone can now be used like a smart card. Together with PKI application running on smart phone, this application can be used to provide 2FA authentication, encryption and digital signature with added usability like biometric protection. For example, a simple windows login, instead of using normal id and password, the computer can pair via Bluetooth with the smart phone with PKI application running. User will only need to authenticate via fingerprint to the smart phone and the user computer will be able to login immediately, without the user having to enter the id and password. This provides added security from shoulder surfing as user did not need to enter the id and password. In addition, it also satisfies 2FA requirements with added security features like biometrics on the phone while taking advantage of PKI security.

Strategies you can consider

When deciding the type of security token to use, you need to consider what is your use cases. If you require 2FA for authentication, there are many choices, either with PKI or without. For example, usage of mobile authenticator can provide 2FA authentication but cannot provide encryption and digital signature functionality. Therefore, if you require authentication, encryption and digital signature, then you will probably need smart card. Then, you need to decide what type of smart card to use. If you are going to use logical and physical security as all-in-one, there are 2 options. You can choose either dual-interface card or hybrid card. You need to check with your physical security vendor on this as well.

Once you decided on using smart card, then you need to consider the type of plastic material you want. There is significant price difference between PET and PVC. In addition, you need to consider the printing of smart card as smart card printer is expensive. You also need to decide whether you want to print the card during issuance of PKI certificates as this can be done via the CMS system. However, you need to check the type and brand of smart card printer supported by the CMS.

Apart from printing, you also need to decide whether you want a FIPS certified smart card or just normal smart card. There are normal commercially available smart card and there is also proprietary smart card. If you choose a proprietary smart card, then you will be at the mercy of the smart card manufacturer. If you choose an open standard smart card features like Personal

Identity Verification (PIV), which is published by NIST, there will be many smart card manufacturers available. In fact, you can also choose USB Token if you company policy allows you to do so.

If you intend to build you own application to interface with the smart card, then you need to check whether the smart card manufacturer provides the middleware that can support PKCS#11 or Crypto API. Some smart card manufacturers charge additional licenses for their middleware. So, you need to be aware of the hidden cost.

If usability is important to you, then you might want to consider having virtual smart card deployment. Some customers that we know, deploy physical smart card for normal office worker and they also deploy virtual smart card for those who needs to travel a lot.

Common issues in PKI implementation

Based on years of experience implementing PKI, here are some common issues in PKI implementation.

PKI Use cases

One reason PKI went into a hype and then failed is that there were no clear use cases defined. Every organization wanted a PKI, but they didn't know why or what the PKI would be used for. Therefore, there is a need to have a clearly defined objective for PKI implementation.

Tracking of Certificates expiry

Authentication, confidentiality, and non-repudiation depend on the validity of PKI certificates. Once a PKI certificate expires, all systems will stop functioning. Therefore, there is a need to clearly define tracking and renewal of certificates. Sufficient time is required to allow the renewal process to take place without impacting users. Software systems can be put in place to scan the entire network to identify soon-to-be-expired certificates and any rough PKIs being deployed.

CDS maintenance

Certificates can be used for authentication, confidentiality, and non-repudiation. Normally, for certificates used for authentication, they should be deleted from the CDS so that authentication applications only see valid authentications in the CDS. Therefore, there is a need to clean up the CDS to ensure that applications can efficiently retrieve the correct information from the CDS.

Key Management and Key rollover

Every certificate has an expiration date attached to it. This is to ensure that when the certificate expires, a new set of keys is generated. This is to prevent hackers from having enough time to hack the keys. For example, if keys take 5 years to hack, then it's a good idea to change the keys every 2-3 years. There is an option to reuse the same keys when the certificate expires. This is called key rollover. However, key rollover is not recommended as hackers may have already compromised the keys. It's better to generate a new set.

Microsoft AD vulnerability

CVE-2022-34691, CVE-2022-26931 and CVE-2022-26923 address an elevation of privilege vulnerability that can occur when the Kerberos Distribution Center (KDC) is servicing a certificate-based authentication request. Before the May 10, 2022 security update, certificate-based authentication would not account for a dollar sign ($) at the end of a machine name. This allowed related certificates to be emulated (spoofed) in various ways. This vulnerability allows normal user to assume domain privileges.

Moving forward, for certificate authentication to work with Microsoft AD, all user's certificate used for authentication must contain the user SID value in the X.509 certificate. The SID has the OID of 1.3.6.1.4.1.311.25.2 which must contain the same value of the user's AD Object SID. If not, the Windows logon using certificate will not work.

For those that already deployed with PKI and could not re-issue user's certificate with SID value, administrator can choose to update the user's entry **altSecurityIdentities** attribute in the AD. The recommended value is:

"X509:<I>IssuerName<SR>1234567890"

For example, if the Certification Authority has the following attributes:

- Issuer: CN=CONTOSO-DC-CA, DC=contoso, DC=com
- SerialNumber: 2B0000000011AC0000000012

The user's **altSecurityIdentities** attribute in AD will have the following value:

- "X509:<I>DC=com,DC=contoso,CN=CONTOSO-DC-CA<SR>1200000000AC11000000002B"

Note that the IssuerName and SerialNumber values are in reverse order.

Index

www.ingramcontent.com/pod-product-compliance
Lightning Source LLC
Chambersburg PA
CBHW051437150726
48000CB00005B/2145

तदबीर से तकदीर

डॉ. मुरलीधर खेतान

First Published in 2021

Becomeshakespeare.com

One Point Six Technologies Pvt Ltd
123, Building J2, Shram Seva Premises, Wadala Truck Depot,
Wadala (East), Mumbai 400037, India
T: +91 8080226699

Copyright © 2021, डॉ. मुरलीधर खेतान

All rights reserved. Any unauthorized reprint or use
of this material is prohibited. No part of this book
may be reproduced or transmitted in any form or
by any means, electronic or mechanical, including photocopying,
recording, or by any information storage and retrieval system
without express written permission from the author/publisher.

Please do not participate in or encourage piracy of copyrighted materials in
violation of the author's rights. Purchase only authorized editions.

©

ISBN - 978-93-5667-732-6

तदबीर से तकदीर

डॉ. मुरलीधर खेतान

YEAR: 1960

CHIEF MINISTER
RAJASTHAN

D.O. No. IRC-2000/Jaipur/539/Sep 5, 2000

Dear Shri Khetan Ji

Rajasthan commenced its journey as a State towards development and progress fifty years ago. Froma backward, feudal conglomeration of Princely States, it has emerged as one of the better governed and progressive states in the country. This has happened, in no small measure, due to the resilience and hard work of its people. Servere and recurring droughts and famines, backwardness and remoteness have not dented the spirit of the Rajasthani. Some of us even went outside the state to excel in a number of fields - business, academics, music, social service... and have made the world a better place for everyone else.

As we celebrate the Golden Jubilee of the State's formation, we recognize your contribution and of all those who have excelled in their chosen fields. To bring together all Rajasthanis who have made a mark in different fields, International Rajasthani Conclave-2000 (IRC-2000) is being organized in Jaipur on 23rd and 24th of September, 2000. This event will provide an insight into the evolution of Rajasthan into a modern State through a series of programs and events.

May I take this opportunity to invite you to participate in IRC-2000 and renew and strengthen your bonds with Rajasthan? We would be happy to receive a confirmation of your presence in the event.

You may find the enclosed information on the event of interest.

With best regards,

Yours sincerely,

(Ashok Gehlot)

Shri Murli Dhar Khetan
Jorhat

मुख्य मंत्री
राजस्थान

23 अक्टूबर 2000

प्रिय श्री खेतान

दीपावली के पर्व पर आप और आपके परिवारजनों के सुखी, समृद्ध और सफल जीवन के लिए मेरी हार्दिक शुभकामनाएं स्वीकार करें।

पिछले माह 23–24 सितम्बर को जयपुर में आयोजित 'अन्तर्राष्ट्रीय राजस्थानी सम्मेलन' में पधार कर आपने इस आयोजन को अपनी उत्साहजनक और सक्रिय उपस्थिति से सफल बनाया। इसके लिए मैं हृदय से आभारी हूँ।

आप लोगों के सुझाव उपयोगी और अमूल्य थे। आपके इन सुझावों व सहयोग के आधार पर हम राजस्थान की आर्थिक और सांस्कृतिक प्रगति के लिए कुछ ठोस प्रयास करना चाहते हैं। 'राजस्थान फाउण्डेशन' की स्थापना इसी दिशा में एक कदम है।

मुझे विश्वास है आपका स्नेह, सौहार्द और सहयोग उत्तरोत्तर और प्रगाढ़ होगा तथा हम मिल–जुल कर राजस्थान को प्रगति के नए आयाम तक ले जाने के अपने स्वप्नों को साकार कर सकेंगे।

आपका स्नेही

(अशोक गहलोत)

श्री मुरलीधर खेतान,
जोरहाट।

8, सिविल लाइन, जयपुर–भारत ● फोन : 381212/381213 (निबास), 380351/380462 (ऑफिस),
फैक्स : 372705 E-mail ; cm@raj.nic.in

Sarbananda Sonowal

Chief Minister, Assam
Guwahati
Dispur
08.01.2021

MESSAGE

I am happy to know that a book on the life and works of eminent businessman, social worker and philanthropist Dr. M.D. khetan Ji is going to be published.

Apart from achieving success in setting up various business which have been providing employment to scores of state's people, Dr. Khetan Ji has also helped in the growth of higher education sector in the State by establishing a world class university in Jorhat. Through his relentless zeal, he has been pursuing many interests with aplomb and also giving back to the society by helping the underprivileged and the needy.

I extend my best wishes on the occasion and I am confident that this book would make the young generation aware about Dr. Khetan Ji's exemplary life and works and inspire them to contribute to the State's overall growth.

(SARBANANDA SONOWAL)

Kumar Sanjay Krishna, IAS
Chief Secretary

GOVERNMENT OF ASSAM
Janata Bhawan, Block-C,
Dispur, Guwahati-781006
Phone : 0361-2261120 (O),
           0361-2261403 (O)
Fax   : 0361-2237200
E-mail : cs-assam@nic.in

FOREWORD

Dr. Murlidhar Khetan's contribution to our state cannot wholly be captured by words on a piece of paper. His contributions far outweigh the reaches of ink. His story is a true reflection of the very essence of our state - a story that speaks of resilience and determination.

As a businessman, Dr. Khetan is a visionary unparalleled. His contribution to power infrastructure in Assam has enabled the development of the state since 1959. His commitment towards ensuring sustainability in the field of power and power infrastructure has remained steadfast over the last 30 years. As the Chairman of the Khetan Group and Neccon Power & Infra Limited, Dr. Khetan's management style and leadership is unique and worth paying attention to. As a result of this, he has won several recognitions and awards, including the coveted National Award for Outstanding Enterpreneurship awarded by the Ministry of Skill Development and Entrepreneurship, Government of India in 1999.

Starting with a meagre salary of Rs. 30/- per month, after having travelled to Assam from Rajasthan in 1950, this business magnate has proved that hardwork, dedication and an entre-prenevrial bent of mind can achieve success, even in the face of adversity. From humble beginnings to the Chairman of the Khetan Group, that has establishments in Power, Tea and Education is truly commendable.

If, however, there is one lesson to learn from this Industrialist's story, it is his contribution towards society and his willingness never to forget his humble beginnings. It was this willingness to give back to the society that manifested in the establishment of The Assam Kaziranga University, which today stands as a beacon of education in the region. The values on which this University stands reflect the image of Dr. Khetan. The gold standard of developing citizens with the consciousness to deliver to society and the creation of an interface between academia and industry that is championed at the Kaziranga University is a matter of pride.

I am glad to learn that Dr. Murlidhar Khetan has decided to pen down this book. It will serve as a great insight into the mind of a great thinker and businessman.

I take this opportunity to wish Dr. Murlidhar Khetan even greater success in the years to come, and good health.

Date: 28.10.2020

(Kumar Sanjay Krishna)

आमुख

डॉक्टर मुरलीधर खेतान इलेक्ट्रिकल जगत के जाने-माने उद्योगपति हैं । उनकी आत्मकथा पढ़ते समय मेरे जेहन में गीतकार आनंद बक्शी का एक गीत रह-रह कर गूंज रहा था । 'तकदीर है क्या, मैं क्या जानूं, मैं आशिक हूं तदबीरों का ।' डॉक्टर खेतान ने तदबीरों से आशिकी न की होती, तो शायद इस मुकाम पर नहीं होते । आधी सदी से भी ज्यादा का सफर वे इस उद्यम में तय कर चुके हैं। राजस्थान के एक छोटे से गांव बानूड़ा से हैं। साधारण परिवार में जन्म लिया, पर आज करोड़ों के टर्नओवर वाली कंपनी के मालिक हैं । वे खेतान ग्रुप और अंतरराष्ट्रीय स्तर की इलेक्ट्रिकल कंपनी 'निकोन पावर एंड इंफ्रा लिमिटेड' के संस्थापक अध्यक्ष और पूर्णकालिक निदेशक हैं। डॉ. खेतान ने इलेक्ट्रिकल व्यवसाय की शुरुआत जोरहाट (असम) से की थी। महज मैट्रिक पास करके १९५० में वे यहां आ गए थे। पहले नौकरी, फिर साझेदारी में इलेक्ट्रिकल उपकरणों का व्यवसाय, इसके बाद १९७९ में हाईटेंशन इलेक्ट्रिकल्स के नाम से स्वतंत्र व्यवसाय की नींव डाली। अपनी सच्चाई, परिश्रम और हिलमिलकर काम करते हुए वे इस उद्यम में सफलता की सीढ़ियां निरंतर चढ़ते गए । आज उनकी कंपनी भारत के पावर सेक्टर में सर्वोच्च शिखर पर है।

चेष्टा, चेष्टा और केवल चेष्टा उनके जीवन का मूल मंत्र रहा है। काम के प्रति निष्ठा को नियति से ज्यादा तरजीह दी है। सच्चाई से काम किया। अपने बिजली उत्पादों में उच्चतम मानदंडों का हमेशा खयाल रखा। तभी गुणवत्ता में वे अन्य कंपनियों से हमेशा आगे रहे। नैतिक मानदंडों का पूरा निर्वाह किया। निर्धारित समय पर माल बनाने और तय तिथि पर उनकी आपूर्ति करने में वे कभी पीछे नहीं रहे। ग्राहकों की जरूरतों के लिए खुद को हमेशा उत्तरदायी समझा। अपनी जिम्मेवारी निभाई ताकि उनके साथ दीर्घकालीन सहभागिता बनी रह सके। उन्हें टर्नकी प्रोजेक्ट्स सहित एचटी/एलटी लाइन का सामान, केबल्स

और कंडक्टर्स बनाने का ५० साल से भी ज्यादा का अनुभव है। उन्होंने अपनी सामाजिक और पर्यावरण संबंधी जिम्मेवारी भी अच्छे से निभाई है ।

शिक्षा के महत्व को समझते हुए उन्होंने २०१२ में जोरहाट में काजीरंगा विश्वविद्यालय की स्थापना की। वे इसके संस्थापक कुलाधिपति हैं । पूर्वोत्तर राज्यों के ग्रामीण और आदिवासी क्षेत्रों में एकल विद्यालय के अभियान को भी उनके प्रयासों से बल मिला।

असम के गौरव डॉक्टर खेतान श्रेष्ठ गुणवत्ता के बिजली उत्पादों के लिए ' द बेस्ट प्रोडक्टिविटी परफोर्मेंस अवार्ड (१९९७)', आउटस्टेंडिंग एंटरप्रिन्योरशिप के लिए नेशनल अवार्ड (१९९९) जैसे कई राष्ट्रीय पुरस्कारों से सम्मानित हो चुके हैं । उदारमना उद्यमी खेतान ने समाज - कल्याण के कई महत्त्वपूर्ण काम किए हैं। उनके इस योगदान को देखते हुए उन्हें १६ सितंबर २०१६ को मंडी गोबिंदगढ़ (जिला फतेहगढ़ साहिब, पंजाब) स्थित देश भगत यूनिवर्सिटी के परिसर में डॉक्ट्रेट की मानद उपाधि से सम्मानित किया गया था । १० दिसंबर २०१७ को जीवनराम मूंगीदेवी गोयनका के चेरिटेबल ट्रस्ट शिलाँग की ओर से भी लाइफटाइम अचीवमेंट अवार्ड दिया गया। वर्ष २००९ में जोरहाट में युवाओं की सबसे पुरानी और अग्रणी संस्था ने 'समाज का गौरव' की उपाधि से अलंकृत किया । उनके व्यक्तित्व की सबसे बड़ी खूबी है सक्रियता । वे ९० साल की वय में भी सक्रिय हैं । तदबीर से तकदीर पर जीत हासिल करने की अपनी कहानी को उन्होंने डायरी में दर्ज किया है । उस समय का सदुपयोग करते हुए जब कोविड-१९ के कारण लॉकडाउन लगा हुआ था। उन्होंने मूलतः अपनी मायड़ बोली में लिखा है । उनके तजुर्बे से व्यवसाय में कदम रखने वाले युवा लाभ ले सकें, इस उम्मीद से उनके अनुभवों को मैंने हिंदी में पुस्तक की शक्ल दी गई है ।

✳ चम्पा शर्मा

सेवानिवृत्त मुख्य उप संपादक,

राजस्थान पत्रिका, जयपुर

खेतानजी की आत्मजीवनी के पृष्ठों से जुड़ना विशेष अनुभव

किसी व्यक्ति के जीवन सफर की दास्तां में कई उतार चढ़ाव और संदेश छिपे होते है। इनमें कुछ प्रेरणादायी संस्मरण होते है तो कुछ हासिल अनुभव । व्यक्ति की जीवनी तब और ज़्यादा खास बन जाती है, जब पारिवारिक, व्यावसायिक और सामाजिक जीवन में शीर्ष पर रह कर समय बिताते हुए व्यक्ति उम्र के शताब्दी दशक में प्रवेश कर जाये । जोरहाट के विशिष्ट उद्यमी और शिक्षाविद डॉक्टर मुरलीधर खेतान इसका जीवंत उदाहरण है। राजस्थान से कर्मभूमि असम आने के बाद जीवनपर्यंत खेतानजी ने जो आदर्श स्थापित किये वे अपने आप में अमूल्य है। संयुक्त परिवार की अवधारणा को कायम रखते हुए वे आज जीवन के नौ दशक बीतने के बाद भी उसी सहज अंदाज़ में नज़र आते है। जीवन में जो सपने उन्होंने देखे, उसे सच करने का माद्दा भी दिखाया। आज उनका कारोबार जोरहाट से गुवाहाटी होते हुए राजस्थान तक फैला है । खेतान परिवार को एक सूत्र में संजोए उन्होंने जीवन के इस उत्तरार्द्ध में अपने जीवन सफर को पन्नों पर उकेरा है । लॉकडाउन की फुर्सत ने उन्हें इस सफर की स्मृतियों को ताजा और लिपिबद्ध करने में मदद की। अपनी आत्मजीवनी में उन्होंने बिना किसी लाग लपेट के हर वो बात साझा की है, जिसका सरोकार उनसे रहा। संपादन के दौरान बरती जाने वाली संपादकीय स्वतंत्रता को छोड़ दें तो इसकी मौलिकता बनाये रखते हुए सभी तथ्यों को किताब में परोसा गया है । वक़्त के पाबंद और गुणवत्ता को प्राथमिकता देने वाले खेतान जी विवादों से सदैव दूर रहे। सही मायनों में उन्हें जोरहाट का नगरसेठ कहा जाए तो अतिश्योक्ति नही होगी । समाज कल्याण और परोपकारिता के क्षेत्र में उन्होंने कभी हाथ पीछे नही खींचे और मुक्त हस्त सहयोग किया । शिक्षा को लेकर उनका जो विज़न था वो आज काजीरंगा विश्वविद्यालय के रूप में नज़र आता

डॉ. मुरलीधर खेतान

है, जहां वे कुलपति के रूप में अपनी सेवाएं दे रहे है । वहीं स्वास्थ्य के क्षेत्र में भी कोई पहल करने की अपनी इच्छा को वे कई बार बयां कर चुके है। उनकी आत्मजीवनी के पृष्ठों से जुड़ कर एक विशेष अनुभव महसूस कर रहा हूँ । आशा है कि यह पुस्तक नई पीढ़ी के लिए मार्गदर्शन का जरिया बनेगी। ईश्वर उन्हें शतायु करें !!

विकास डिडवानिया

सहायक संपादक

प्रस्तावना

कोविड - १९ का सबसे पहला मरीज दिसंबर २०१९ में चीन के वुहान शहर में सामने आया । इसके बाद यह भारत सहित विश्व के सभी देशों में तेजी से फैला। इस महामारी से पूरी दुनिया में शुरू हुआ मौतों का सिलसिला अभी थमा नहीं है । जीवन जरूर थम सा गया है । संक्रमण न फैले, इसके लिए लॉकडाउन लगा हुआ है। सबके काम-धंधे ठप पड़े हुए हैं । मेरे अपने व्यवसाय पर भी फिलहाल विराम लगा हुआ है । ९० की उम्र पार कर चुका हूं । हमेशा सक्रिय रहा हूँ। इतने लंबे सफर में मैंने कई उतार- चढ़ाव देखे हैं । खट्टे-मीठे अनुभव हुए हैं। जीवन के पिछले पन्नों को खोलता हूं तो हैरानी होती है, जमाने में कितना अंतर आ गया है। कई नई बातें हमारी जीवन शैली में जुड़ गई हैं, तो कई पुरानी अच्छी बातों को हम भूल गए हैं। सीकर के बानूड़ा गांव से हूँ । मामूली परिवार से । रोजी-रोटी के लिए मेरा गांव छूटा। राजस्थान से असम जाकर बसना पड़ा। आज मैं खेतान ग्रुप और अंतरराष्ट्रीय स्तर की इलेक्ट्रिकल कंपनी 'निकोन पावर एंड इंफ्रा लिमिटेड' का संस्थापक अध्यक्ष हूँ, पूर्णकालिक निदेशक हूँ । काजीरंगा विश्वविद्यालय का संस्थापक कुलाधिपति भी हूँ । प्रतिवर्ष करोड़ों का टर्नओवर है। यहां तक पहुंचने की मेरी यात्रा आसान नहीं थी । मुझे बहुत संघर्ष करने पड़े हैं। पर मैं पीछे नहीं हटा। हार कर बैठ जाना मेरी फितरत में नहीं था । सतत चेष्टा से किया गया उद्योग कभी कहीं निष्फल नहीं होता। मैंने हमेशा नियति से ज्यादा निष्ठा को तरजीह दी है। परिवार और मित्रों को साथ लेकर चला हूँ । तभी इस मुकाम तक पहुंच पाया हूँ। तदबीर से तकदीर की मेरी कहानी व्यवसाय - जगत में कदम रखने वाले युवाओं के शायद कुछ काम आ सके। इसी मकसद से मैंने लॉकडाउन के दौरान, ५ फरवरी २०२० से अपने अनुभवों को अल्फाज देना शुरू किया।

डॉ. मुरलीधर खेतान

मेरा जन्म १० नवम्बर १९३१ का है, हालांकि निश्चित तौर पर नहीं कह सकता कि यही तारीख है । उस समय जन्मदिन मनाने का चलन नहीं था, न ही किसी सरकारी विभाग में जन्म-मरण का पंजीकरण होता था । सरकार की तरफ से भी इसकी मांग नहीं होती थी । उस समय भारत पर अंग्रेजों का राज था। देश करीब ६०० रियासतों में बंटा हुआ था । न बिक्री कर, न आय कर और न ही काला - सफेद रुपयों का हिसाब । जो जिसके पास था, सब सफेद ही था । न कोई सरकारी अस्पताल था और न ही सरकारी पाठशालाएं थीं। मैं ३-४ साल का हुआ तब तक मेरे पिताजी, छोटे और बड़े ताऊजी सब एक ही हवेली में रहते थे । एक ही रसोई में खाना बनता । रसोई में ही बैठ कर खाते। मेरे बड़े ताऊजी का चेहरा मुझे धुंधला- सा याद है। कम आयु में ही उनका देहांत हो गया था। उनके बाद बड़ी ताईजी भी महाप्रयाण कर गईं। छोटे ताऊजी, छोटी ताईजी, पिताजी, मेरी माँ तथा सभी भाभियां साथ ही रहते थे। उस वक्त हवेलियां बड़ी होती थीं । उनमें एक चौक होता था। आज भी गांवों में (और शहरों में भी) चौक वाले मकान मिल जाते हैं। मुझे याद है, जब मैं ४ साल का हुआ, हमारा परिवार अलग हो गया। छोटे-बड़े ताऊजी का परिवार इसी हवेली में रह गये और मेरे पिताजी हवेली के पीछे बने नए घर में चले गए।

उस घर से इस घर हम अपना सामान लाये थे, वह मुझे थोड़ा-थोड़ा याद है । बानूड़ा गांव, खूड़ रियासत में था। इसलिए हमारे गांव को अब भी खूड़ बानूड़ा कहते हैं । हमारे राजा के पास कुल १२ गांव की रियासत थी और उनका मुख्यालय हमारे गांव से दो मील दूर खूड़ था। सभी गांव १० मील के दायरे में थे। एक गांव से दूसरा गांव १० मील से ज्यादा दूरी पर नहीं था। बल्कि दूरी इससे भी कम होती थी ।

जैसे तैसे मैट्रिक की

६ साल का हुआ तब मुझे गांव की स्कूल में बैठाया गया । स्कूल हमारे राजाजी की तरफ से चलती थी। उसमें एक ही मास्टर था, जिन्हें हम गुरुजी बुलाते थे । वे ही सारे विषय पढ़ाते थे । अंग्रेजी हमारी स्कूल में नहीं थी ।

न ज्यादा किताबें होती थीं। एक ही किताब से सारी पढ़ाई करवाते थे । हमारी स्कूल में एक ही कमरा था। पढ़ने वाले कम्प्युटर्सची ३०-४० बच्चे । कमरा छोटा पड़ता था । इसलिए गुरुजी स्कूल के सामने पीपल के एक बड़े पेड़ के नीचे

जमीन पर बैठाकर पढ़ाते थे । गणित की कोई किताब नहीं होती थी । गुरुजी गिनती, गुणा - भाग सब मुखजबानी पढ़ाते थे । मुखजबानी ही पूछते थे । हमें तुरन्त जवाब देना पड़ता था । सही हुआ तो ठीक, वरना डंडे पड़ते थे ।

अध्यापक की नियुक्ति राजा की तरफ से होती थी। वेतन पांच रुपया महीना। स्कूल के बच्चे बारी-बारी से गुरुजी के घर उनकी जरूरत का सीधा यानी आटा, दाल, मसाला, गुड़-शक्कर वगैरह दे आते थे। उससे उन्हें सहारा लग जाता था। होली, दीवाली, चतड़ा चौथ (गणेश चतुर्थी) जैसे त्योहारों पर उन्हें एक-एक रुपया भेंट भी करते थे । पर वे ही जिनकी देने की सामर्थ्य होती थी। इस तरह उन्हें साल में ५०-६० रुपए और मिल जाते थे । सेठों की प्राइवेट पाठशालाओं में अध्यापक को सेठ ही तनख्वाह देते थे । लड़कों को कुछ नहीं देना पड़ता था । किन्तु छोटे गांवों में सेठों की पाठशालाएं नहीं के

बराबर होती थीं। जब मैं १० - १२ साल का हुआ, स्कूल की पढ़ाई पूरी हो गई और हम घर का काम करने लगे । १९४४ में हमारे गांव में गंगाबक्शजी कानोड़िया ने एक मिडिल स्कूल खोली । मैंने वहां आठवीं तक की पढ़ाई की। १९४७ में देश आजाद होने के बाद वह स्कूल सरकारी हो गया ।

उस जमाने में २-३ घंटे से ज्यादा पढ़ाई नहीं होती थी । पढ़ाई के बाद बड़े लड़के घर के काम में लग जाते थे । ५ से ८ साल तक के खेलते रहते । हम पीपल के पेड़ के नीचे या उसके आसपास खुली जगह पर खेलते थे। कबड्डी, खो-खो, क्रिकेट । क्रिकेट आज जैसा  नहीं था। उसे केवल दो खिलाड़ी खेलते थे । दर्जी से फटे-पुराने कपड़ों की एक गेंद बनवा लेते थे । रेत के करीब एक फुट ऊंचे गोल ढेले पर एक डंडा रोप दिया जाता। एक लड़का गेंद फेंकता और दूसरा लड़का उस डंडे को उखड़ने से बचाने की कोशिश करता । डंडा उखड़ने पर लड़का आउट हो जाता था। वह गेंद फेंकने आ जाता और दूसरे लड़के की बारी डंडे को उखड़ने से बचाने की हो जाती थी । यह खेल आधा घंटा या ज्यादा भी चलता था। दोनों लड़कों की सहमति से । समय की कोई पाबंदी नहीं थी। उसके अलावा रुमाल से भी खेलते थे । गोल घेरा बना कर दस-बीस लड़के बैठ जाते थे। एक लड़का कपड़े के टुकड़े या रुमाल लेकर घेरे का चक्कर लगाता हुआ दौड़ता था । वह चुपके से किसी लड़के के पीछे रुमाल रख देता । उस लड़के को मालूम चलने पर वह उस रुमाल को लेकर दौड़ने लगता था। पता नहीं चलने पर उसे मार खानी पड़ती थी। वैसे रुमाल उस जमाने में कम ही मिलता था । चिथड़ों से ही खेलना पड़ता था ।

गांव में हमारी दुकान थी । किराने के अलावा कपड़ा और अन्य सामान भी रखते थे। शाम तक १५ - २० रुपए का ही सामान बिक पाता था । कमाई ज्यादा नहीं होने से घर का खर्चा मुश्किल से चल रहा था। हमारे गांव से सीकर

१४ मील दूर था । १९४८ में हमने सीकर में तबेला रोड पर सरावगी की नसीयां के पास एक दुकान ली। धान, गुड़, शक्कर सब रखते और आढ़त का काम भी करते । सबसे बड़े भाईसाहब सुआलालजी और मैं उस दुकान को संभाल रहे थे । एक दिन मैं किसी काम से संघ कार्यालय गया था। वहां एक सज्जन ने मुझे २-३ घंटे रोज कार्यालय आने का सुझाव दिया। कहा, यहां तुम्हारी मैट्रिक की पढ़ाई

भी हो जाएगी, और शाखा भी आते रहना। घंटाघर स्थित संघ कार्यालय में शाम को शाखा लगती थी । मेरे अलावा तीन और लड़के थे। शांतिलाल जैन (दूजोद), रामस्वरूप जोगानी (सीकर), और भंवर सिंह (दाधिया) । तीन घंटे पढ़ने के बाद हम चारों रोज शाखा जाते थे । संघ से मेरे जुड़ाव की कहानी यहीं से शुरू हुई । कार्यालय में कभी-कभी भैरोंसिंहजी शेखावत आते थे। वे हमें राजनीति पढ़ाते । संघ के जिला प्रचारक भंवरसिंहजी शेखावत अंग्रेजी, मोतीसिंह राठौड़ हिंदी और परसरामजी अग्रवाल (वकील, रघुनाथगढ़) गणित पढ़ाते थे । भैरोंसिंहजी शेखावत का स्नेह मुझे बाद में भी मिलता रहा । उनके सान्निध्य में मैंने राजनीति के गुर सीखे। १९५० में मैंने मैट्रिक की प्राइवेट परीक्षा दी और प्रथम श्रेणी से पास हुआ ।

जीविका के लिए जोरहाट

हम पांच भाई थे, दो मुझसे बड़े और दो छोटे । सुवालाल जी और बंशीधर जी मुझसे बड़े थे । नेमीचंद और प्रेमसुख छोटे । बंशीधर भाईसाहब पक्के कांग्रेसी थे और खादी पहनते थे । गांव के लोग उन्हें नेहरूजी बुलाते थे। हम पांचों भाई साथ रहते थे। तीन बहनें थीं। तीन में गुलाबी जीजी सब बहन-भाइयों में बड़ी थीं। दूसरी तीसरे नम्बर पर थीं बिदामी जीजी, बंशीधर भाईसाहब से छोटी । और तीसरी गीता सातवें नम्बर पर, नेमीचंद से छोटी। सुवालाल भाईसाहब (दांतारामगढ़ भूरिया के यहां), गुलाबी जीजी और बिदामी जीजी की शादी मेरे जन्म से पहले ही हो गई थी । बंशीधर भाई की शादी मेरे जन्म के करीब ५ साल बाद हुई । मेरी शादी सन् १९५० में ६ जून को सुरेरा मंढा में महादेवजी बंसल की पुत्री सोहनी देवी खेतान से हुई थी । जेठ का तपता महीना था, न बिजली, न पंखा । बीजणी (पंखी) से ही हवा करते थे । हर बराती को बीजणी दी जाती थी ।

मेरे बाद १९५३ में छोटे भाई नेमीचन्द की (नेछवा में मालीराम जी मीठड़ी वालों के यहां), १९५८ में तीसरे नंबर की बहन गीता और १९५८ में ही १५ जून को सबसे छोटे भाई प्रेमसुख की (खोरंडी गांव में विहारीलाल जी

                                                  डॉ. मुरलीधर खेतान

दुर्गादत्त के घर) हुई। बहनों की शादी की तारीखें याद नहीं हैं। खीरोड़ गांव के एक ही परिवार में चाचा-ताऊ के यहां हुई थी। दो बहनें तो दो सगे भाइयों को ही दी थीं। इस तरह १९५८ तक शादी-ब्याह के काम निपट गए थे ।

हमारा संयुक्त परिवार था । हम सब गांव में एक ही हवेली में रहते थे, वहीं सोते, वहीं खाते। एक ही रसोई में सबका खाना बनता । सब जने रसोई में ही बारी-बारी से जीमते । किसी के भी मन में कोई मनमुटाव नहीं था । सब प्रेम से रहते थे। अपनापन था। अनाज अपने खेत से मिल जाता था । ग्वार-मोठ कम ही चलता था । बाजरा ही ज्यादा खाते थे। कभी-कभी गेहूँ के फलके बनते, तो वो भी मिल जाते । घर में गाय, भैंस, ऊंट, बैल, बकरी सब थे। दूध, दही, छाछ, घी की कमी नहीं थी । छाछ ज्यादा होती, पड़ोस में दे देते। इस प्रकार जीवन की गाड़ी चल रही थी। गांव की दुकान पर बंशीधर भाईसाहब रहते और सीकर वाली दुकान मैं और सुवालाल जी भाईसाहब संभाल रहे थे। परिवार बढ़ा, तो खर्चे भी बढ़े। गांव और सीकर की दुकानों से गुजारा नहीं हो रहा था। शादी-ब्याह आदि मौकों पर ब्याज पर पैसे लेने पड़ते थे । एक दिन हम सबने मिल बैठकर विचार किया कि हम में से किसी को गांव से बाहर जाकर नौकरी करनी चाहिए । असम या कलकत्ता (कोलकाता) कहीं भी । इससे घर को सहारा लगेगा। सबने मुझे जोरहाट भेजना तय किया । जोरहाट में हमारे एक संबंधी रहते थे, जेसराम जीवनराम जालान । मैं १९५० में जोरहाट आ गया । महीना मुझे याद नहीं है। औरतें गांव या सीकर रहती थीं। जोरहाट से पहले मैंने जयपुर में भी काम किया था। सीकर में रामस्वरूपजी नंदलालजी काबरा और हमारी दुकान अगल-बगल में थी । नंदलालजी काबरा ने सुझाव दिया कि चूंकि सीकर में हमारा काम सही नहीं चल रहा है, मैं उनकी जयपुर की दुकान सागरमल सत्यनारायण फर्म को संभाल लूं। उनके चीनी, तेल, घी वगैरह का थोक का काम था। उनके कहने पर मुझे वहां भेज दिया गया। मैंने वहां १० - १२ महीने खूव मन लगाकर काम किया। पर जोग संस्कार जोरहाट का था । दाना-पानी वहीं का लिखा था।

बानूड़ा से जोरहाट बेहद थका देने वाला लंबा सफर था। सीकर से गुवाहाटी करीब २०३८ किमी और गुवाहाटी से जोरहाट करीब ३१० किमी ।

कुल २३४८ किमी । पहुंचने में करीब १२ - १३ दिन लग गए थे। मां ने रास्ते के लिए लड्डू, पेठे, नमकीन और २-३ दिन चल सके उतने मोयन के परांठे बना दिए । मोयन की रोटी जल्दी खराब नहीं होती है। साथ में अचार और हरी मिर्च भी । मेरे लिए तीन गंजी, तीन कमीज और तीन पायजामे दर्जी से सिलवा दिए। तब सिलाई नग के हिसाब से नहीं देनी पड़ती थी। साल के ११ रुपए बंधे हुए थे, जितने चाहो सिलवाओ। एक बैडिंग (होल्डोल स्लीपिंग बैग) घर में ही रखा था, उसमें एक पतला गदा, एक पतला तकिया और एक कंबल डाल लिए। कपड़े भी उसी में रख लिए । रास्ते के लिए मैंने पुराने कपड़े पहन लिए । एक छबड़ी में खाने का सारा सामान पैक करके उसे कपड़े से बांध दिया। घर से रवाना होने से पहले बड़ों का आशीर्वाद लिया । ताऊजी के घर जाकर भी उनकी आशीष ली । आशीर्वाद का एक-एक रुपया करके १४ रुपये हो गये थे । फिर गांव के श्रीजानकीवल्लभजी के मन्दिर में दर्शन कर आशीर्वाद लिया। एक रुपया पुजारीजी को भेंट किया । हम रात १० बजे किसी परिचित के घर आ गये थे । मुहूर्त सुबह ४ बजे का था । ३ बजे उठकर नित्यकर्म से निवृत्त हुआ । ४ बजे गांव से मांडोता पैदल ही रवाना हो गये। मांडोता डेढ़ मील दूर था । हम करीब ६ बजे वहां पहुंच गये । सुवालाल जी भाईसाहब ऊंट पर हमारा सामान लेकर ७ बजे मांडोता पहुंचे। हम यहां गुलाबचन्दजी मदनलालजी छाबड़ा के यहां रुके। चाय-नाश्ता करके १० बजे भाई के साथ खाना खाया। ११ बजे ऊंट पर बैठ कर सीकर के लिए रवाना हो गये। सीकर दो- तीन बजे पहुंचे। वहां कन्हैयालाल कुन्दलमलजी मालपाणी के यहां ठहरे। गाड़ी का समय रात ९ बजे का था । कन्हैयालाल कुन्दनमलजी का बेटा गणेशलाल मालपाणी मेरे जिगरी दोस्तों में है। हम शाम साढ़े सात बजे तांगे डॉ. मुरलीधर खेतान

से सीकर रेलवे स्टेशन पहुंच गये। टिकट चैक करवाकर गाड़ी के डिब्बे में ८ बजे ही बैठकर अपनी सीट पक्की कर ली। साथ में खंडेला के भाईसाहब दुर्गादत्तजी थे । उनको शिवसागर जाना था। शिवसागर जोरहाट से ३० मील है। दोनों का रास्ता एक ही था । वही गाड़ी जाती है। गाड़ी ठीक ८५५ पर रवाना हो गई। उस समय डीजल के इंजन तो थे नहीं। कोयले से गाड़ी चलती थी सो पहुंचते-पहुंचते उसकी कालिख से काले भूत-से दिखने लगे थे । गाड़ी

अगले दिन सुबह पांच बजकर ग्यारह मिनट पर दिल्ली रेलवे स्टेशन पहुंच गई। हम वहीं प्लेटफॉर्म पर बैडिंग खोलकर लेट गए। एक- एक करके नित्यकर्म से निवृत्त हुए। फिर चाय मंगवा कर अचार - परांठों का नाश्ता किया। पिकनिक - सा आनन्द आया । दिल्ली से कानपुर गाड़ी शाम ७ बजे जाती थी, सो दिन भर प्लेटफॉर्म पर ही पड़े रहे। कोई वेटिंग रूम वगैरह नहीं था। शाम ७ बजे दिल्ली से कानपुर रवाना हुए। कानपुर में रात ११ बजे गाड़ी खाली हो गई। हमने यहां भी प्लेटफॉर्म पर बैडिंग खोला और लेट गए। यहां से बरौनी की गाड़ी सुबह १० बजे मिलती थी, जो रात ८ बजे वहां जाकर खाली हो जाती थी । बरौनी पहुंच कर प्लेटफॉर्म पर ही रात बिताई। जो घर से लाया था, खाया। कभी-कभी गर्म पूड़ी सब्जी स्टेशन से ले लेते थे ।

बरौनी से गंगा नदी जहाज से पार करनी पड़ती थी । जहाज मिलने तक बरौनी स्टेशन पर ही रहे । जहाज से बरौनी घाट जाकर बरौनी स्टेशन (गंगा नंदी के दूसरी तरफ) । प्लेटफॉर्म पर फिर बैडिंग खोला और लेट गए। दूसरे दिन सुबह १० बजे बरौनी से कटिहार की गाड़ी मिली, जो रात ९ बजे सिलीगुड़ी पहुंची। सिलीगुड़ी में एक मारवाड़ी बासा (ढाबा) था । वहां खाना खाकर सिलीगुड़ी स्टेशन आकर सो गए। वहां से अगले दिन गाड़ी से अमीनगांव ब्रह्मपुत्र घाट पर शाम ४-५ बजे पहुंचे। रातभर अमीनगांव रेलवे स्टेशन पर रहे। दूसरे दिन सुबह ब्रह्मपुत्र घाट से जहाज में बैठकर शाम ३-४ बजे गुवाहाटी घाट पहुंचे। उस समय रात में गाड़ियां बहुत कम चलती थीं ।

दिन में भी १०० किलोमीटर से ज्यादा नहीं चलती थीं। अगले दिन सुबह गुवाहाटी होते हुए शाम को मरियानी रेलवे स्टेशन पहुंचे। रात में जोरहाट जाने का साधन नहीं मिला । मरियानी में ही प्लेटफार्म पर रात बितानी पड़ी। अगले सन् १९५० जोरहाट जं: गजठक्अढ गक दिन सुबह जोरहाट के (उ) लिए टैक्सी ली और ११ बजे वहां पहुंच गए। उस समय रास्ते खराब थे । गाड़ियां भी पुरानी थीं। एक घंटा लग जाता था । अब तो आधा ही समय लगता है । आखिर अपने गंतव्य पर पहुंच ही गया । जोरहाट में अपने संबंधी जेसराम जीवनराम जालान के यहां रुका। सफर में मेरे कपड़ों और शरीर पर कालिख जम गई थी। सबसे पहले नहाया, कपड़े धोए। फिर खाना खाकर कमरे में जाकर

लेट गया। थका हुआ तो था ही, लेटते ही नींद आ गई । जालानजी अपने काम पर चले गए थे। रात ८ - ९ बजे खाना खाते समय जालानजी के पास किसी दुकानदार का फोन आया। दुकानदार ने कहा, आपके यहां देस से एक लड़का आया है । जालानजी बोले, हां, पर वह बणियों का बेटा है। कामकाज

में अभी नया ही है । दुकानदार ने कहा, नए की कोई बात नहीं है, लड़का अच्छे घर-घराने का ईमानदार और मेहनती होना चाहिए। तब जालानजी ने कहा, लड़का अच्छे घराने का है, मैं जिम्मेदारी लेता हूं। उनका जवाब था, लड़के को भेज दो । काम करने को लेकर मैं बहुत ही उत्सुक था और बेसब्र भी । मैं रात को ही उनके यहां पहुंच गया। उनकी दुकान नजदीक ही थी। वहीं रहने का प्रबंध था। फर्म का नाम था गार्डन स्टोर्स प्राइवेट लिमिटेड और मालिक थे इमनादत्तजी जालान ।

पहली नौकरी

१९४५ में द्वितीय विश्व युद्ध समाप्त हो गया था । सेना गैरजरूरी सामान की नीलामी कर रही थी । इमनादत्तजी ने लगभग पांच सौ क्विंटल लोहे के नट बोल्ट खरीद लिए थे। दुकान पर यूपी का एक और लड़का था- मदन मोहन । नट बोल्टों को साइज के हिसाब से छांट कर ५०-५० सेर की ढेरी बनानी थी। साफ करके तेल भी लगाना था । दरमाहा (मासिक वेतन) था ३० रुपए महीना । खाना रहना, बाकी सारा खर्च उनका था । मैं जी जान से काम में लग गया। एक दिन इमनादत्तजी के बेटे को काम से बाहर जाना पड़ा। इमनादत्तजी बोले, लालाबाबू तो है नहीं, आप रोकड़ (कैश) के ताला लगा देना । वह कल आएगा तब हिसाब मिला लेगा । मैं बोला, रोकड़ तो मैं मिला दूंगा। मैंने रोकड़ खाता-बही का काम किया हुआ है । वे बोले, ठीक है, रोकड़ मिलाकर पन्ना मुझे दिखाओ। रोकड़ मिलाकर मैंने उन्हें पन्ना दिखा दिया । २-३ पैसों का फर्क था । बे बोले, पान मंगवाया था, वह तो लिखा ही नहीं । उसे लिख कर मैंने हिसाब दिया तो इमनादत्तजी बोले, कल से तू बही-खाता का काम किया कर । उन्होंने मुझसे पूछा, तलपट (बैलेंस शीट) मिलाना आता है ? मैं बोला, जी आता है । तो वे बोले, कल से बही-खाते का काम पूरा करके तलपट मिला देना। कल से तेरी तनख्वाह १०० रुपया महीना है । मन लगा कर काम करेगा तो दरमाहा और बढ़ जाएगा। मैंने बारह महीनों के खाते का काम ३-४ महीने में पूरा करके तलपट बना दिया और इमनादत्तजी को सौंप दिया। वे मेरे काम से खुश थे। अब वे मुझे अपने साथ चाय बागान भी ले जाने लगे। वहां माल की डिलिवरी, बिल पास करवाना, नए माल का ऑर्डर और पेमेंट का चेक आदि काम १२-१ बजे तक पूरा कर लेता। घर लौट कर खाना खाता और गार्डन स्टोर्स के बही-खातों का काम निपटाने बैठ जाता। दिन में लेटने तक

की फुर्सत नहीं मिलती थी। पर हां, रात १० बजे तक सब सो जाते थे। जब रामनवमी आई तो मैं इमनादत्तजी से बोला, मैं आपका बताया सारा काम कर रहा हूं । मेरा दरमाहा बढ़ना चाहिए। वे बोले, कल रामनवमी पर दरमाहे का जमा खर्च हो जाये तब देख लेना। दूसरे दिन जब मैंने बही-खाता देखा तो रोकड़ में मेरा दरमाहा रामनवमी से २५१ रुपए जमा खर्च किया हुआ था। १९५० में जब मैं जोरहाट आया था, उसी साल अगस्त के महीने में असम में बहुत तेज भूकंप आया था। रिक्टर स्केल पर इसकी तीव्रता ८.६ थी । इस त्रासदी में कई लोग मारे गए। जान-माल का बहुत नुकसान हुआ । घरवालों को चिंता हो गई। भाईसाहब ने घर लौट आने का तार भेज दिया । मैंने जवाबी तार दिया कि भूकंप थम गया है। अब कोई डर नहीं है । भूकंप के झटके १०-१५ दिन तक आते रहे। इस दौरान हमने कई रातें दुकान के सामने एक ट्रक में बिताई थीं। दूसरी रामनवमी आने पर मैंने इमनादत्तजी से घर जाने की अनुमति मांगी और कहा कि दो महीने में लौट आऊंगा । वे बोले, तेरा दरमाहा ५०१ रुपए महीना कर दिया है। देस में ज्यादा मत रुकना । मैं बोला, दो महीने से ज्यादा नहीं रहूंगा। जाने-आने का टाइम तो लगेगा ही । जोरहाट में करीब तीन साल रहने के बाद १९५३ में चौमासे में अपने गांव आ सका । उसके बाद जोरहाट जाने-आने का क्रम बना रहा और मेरा वेतन भी बढ़ता रहा ।

असम से जब भी राजस्थान आता, हम ४-५ लड़के होते थे। वापस भी साथ ही जाते थे। अमीनगांव घाट पर जो गाड़ी आती, वह सिलीगुड़ी ५-६ बजे शाम को पहुंचती और दूसरे दिन सुबह ७-८ बजे आगे चलती । सिलीगुड़ी में एक मारवाड़ी ढाबा था । उस समय खाने के सिर्फ ५०-६० पैसे लगते थे। खाना खाने के बाद जब हमने पापड़ मांगा, तो ढाबेवाला बोला, पापड़ के अलग से पैसे लगेंगे। हमारे साथ का एक लड़का बड़ा उस्ताद था । बोला, 'पापड़ का दाम लगेगा, फलकों का तो नहीं ना । तो फलके ही आने दो।' हम जिद में २० - २५ फलके और खा गए। अंत में दुखी होकर ढाबेवाले ने कहा, 'पापड़ ही ले लो भाई लोगो और खाना निपटाओ । पापड़ के पैसे नहीं लूंगा। अब तो खुश ।' तब जाकर हम माने ।

सीकर पहुंचकर अपने-अपने गांव जाने से पहले हम सब सीकर की एक धर्मशाला में रुके। वहां नहा-धोकर कपड़े बदले । फिर अपने-अपने गांव के लिए निकले । बानूड़ा के लिए बस चांदपोल गेट से शाम पांच बजे जाती थी। घर के लिए फल-सब्जी लेकर बस में बैठा और ६ बजे बानूड़ा पहुंचा। करीब तीन साल से लौटा था । मेरे घर के और गांव के काफी लोग बस पर ही मिलने आ गए थे। मैंने अपना सामान उनके साथ भेज दिया और मैं गांव में सबसे मिलता-मिलाता घर पहुंचा। इस तरह जोरहाट में अपने पहले प्रवास के बाद १९५३ में आषाढ़ के महीने में घर पहुंचा। गांव के बाजार में एक बड़ा बरगद का पेड़ था । बस यहीं रुकती थी । बस अड्डा अलग से नहीं था। एक चबूतरे पर बैठकर लोग बस की प्रतीक्षा करते थे । खाना खाने के बाद इसी चबूतरे पर हम दोस्तों के साथ ताश खेलते थे । मेरे साथियों में ग्राम सेवक हरिराम सोनी, बलदेव सुनार, महावीर पहाड़िया, पन्नालाल बैद. आचार्य रामनिवास शर्मा, बसेसरलाल शर्मा, बद्रीप्रसाद भूत, रामनिवास भूत, मंगनीराम शर्मा और महावीर शर्मा आदि थे। इनमें से अब ज्यादातर नहीं रहे। कुछ अस्वस्थ हैं। साथियों का वह दौर याद करता हूं तो आंखें नम हो जाती हैं ।

पहले कर्जा उतारा

जोरहाट जाने से पहले २५-३० हजार रुपए की देनदारी थी । एक दिन सब भाइयों ने मशविरा किया कि केवल नौकरी से तो देनदारी चूकेगी नहीं। हमें आमदनी का जरिया बढ़ाना चाहिए। मैं छोटे भाई नेमीचन्द को अपने साथ असम ले आया और डिब्रूगढ़ में नंदलालजी तोदी के यहां नौकरी लगवा दी। इस बीच बड़े भाईसाहब ने कहा कि राजस्थान से मूंग असम जाते हैं। एक गाड़ी पर ४-५ हजार रुपए तक मुनाफा बैठ जाता है। उन्होंने सीकर से मूंग की गाड़ियां जोरहाट भेजने की बात कही और कहा कि वहां ऐसा कोई हो जो मालगाड़ी की बिल्टी बैंक से छुड़वाकर उसे बेचे और हमारा मुनाफा हमें देदे । इससे अपना कर्जा चुक सकता है। मैंने कहा, मैं जोरहाट जाकर इमनादत्तजी से बात करके बताऊंगा क्योंकि मैं वहां किसी को नहीं जानता । भाईजी बोले, ठीक है । भादो में शाद्ध लगने से पहले मैं जोरहाट लौट आया । इमनादत्तजी को भाईजी की सारी बात बताई । वे बोले, मैं तुम्हारा यह काम करवा दूंगा । मारवाड़ी पट्टी में एपी रावतमल फर्म के मालिक हमीरचन्दजी पींचा इमनादत्तजी के घनिष्ठ मित्र थे । उन्होंने हमीरचंदजी को पूरी बात बताते हुए कहा कि आप तो बस मूंगों की गाड़ियों की बिल्टी बैंक से छुड़ाकर मूंग बेच देना । नफा-नुकसान की चिंता मत करना। मैंने भाईजी को तार दिया कि आप एपी राबतमल मारवाड़ी पट्टी के नाम से मूंग की ४-५ गाड़ियों की बिल्टी बैंक में भेज कर मुझे तार कर देना । इमनादत्तजी ने काम की जबान दे दी है। भाईजी ने ९-१० दिन बाद मूंग की पांच गाड़ियां भेजकर मुझे तार से सूचना दे दी। मैंने इमनादत्तजी को इतला की कि मूंग की ५ गाड़ियां भाईजी ने सीकर से भेज दी हैं। बिल्टी हमीरचंदजी के फर्म के नाम से है। आप उन्हें कह दें। उन्होंने हमीरचंदजी से बैंक से बिल्टी छुड़वाकर माल को सही भाव पर बेच कर हिसाब भेजने को

  डॉ. मुरलीधर खेतान

कह दिया । हमीरचन्दजी बोले ठीक है । बात आई गयी हो गई। उन्होंने बिल्टी छुड़ाकर अपने पास रख ली, पर माल नहीं पहुंचा । १५-२० दिन बाद हमीरचंदजी इमनादत्तजी के पास आये और बोले, अरे इमनादत, तेरे मुनीम की मूंग की गाड़ियां तो आई ही नहीं । दरअसल हुआ यह था कि सिलीगुड़ी के पास रेलवे पुल टूटने से माल वहीं फंस गया था । इमनादत्तजी बोले, मूंगों के डिब्बे सिलीगुड़ी में ही पड़े हैं, तो अब क्या किया जाए । हमीरचंदजी बोले, मूंग तो आए नहीं हैं, बाजार में लोग मूंगों की बिल्टी मांग रहे हैं। मैंने पूछा, क्या भाव में मांग रहे हैं? उन्होंने बताया, एक बिल्टी पर चार हजार रुपए दे रहे हैं। मैंने पांच हजार मांगे हैं । साढ़े चार हजार तक मिल जाने चाहिए। मैंने कहा, बिल्टी आज ही बेच दीजिए। बिल्टी रखना ठीक नहीं है। पता नहीं कब पुल ठीक होगा और कब मूंग पहुंचेंगे। यह बात १९५४-५५ की है। शाम को हमीरचंदजी इमनादत्तजी के पास वापस आए और बोले, तेरे मुनीम के मूंगों की बिल्टी बेच दी है । ४६०० रुपए प्रति बिल्टी मिले हैं। इन रुपयों का क्या करना है । इमनादत्तजी बोले, तुम अपना कमीशन काट लो और बाकी पैसे मेरे मुनीम को दे दो। दूसरे दिन बिल्टी का हिसाब और २३ हजार रुपए लाकर दे दिए। मैंने कहा, हमें यह रुपया सीकर भेजना है, आप बताएं कैसे भेज सकते हैं । हमीरचंदजी बोले, मुझे राजस्थान से अपने रुपए मंगवाने हैं। ऐसे में मैं तुम्हें ये रुपए वहीं दिलवा देता हूं। लेकिन रुपए सरदारशहर से लेने पड़ेंगे। मैंने हामी भर ली। उन्होंने तेईस हजार रुपए देने का कागज लिखकर दे दिया । पैसों के लेन-देन का यह देसी तरीका आज भी चलता है । मैंने वह कागज भाईसाहब को भेज दिया । १०-१५ दिनों में कागज पहुंचा, तो वे बड़े खुश हुए। रुपये मिलने पर सबसे पहले कर्जा चुकाया । सिर से भार उतरा। हालांकि परिवार बढ़ने से खर्चे भी बढ़ गए थे। मेरी और नेमीचंद की नौकरी से घर का खर्चा तो चल रहा था। लेकिन अन्य ऊपरी खर्चों में दिक्कतें आती थीं। परिवार में

शादी-ब्याह का खर्चा, बहन-बेटियों के यहां शादियों में मायरा भरना और बच्चे के जन्म पर न्हाण (प्रसूता का पहला स्नान), जलवा पूजन, नामकरण आदि खर्चे मध्यम परिवार के लिए भारी पड़ जाते थे। गांव में चन्दा वगैरह भी मौके पर देना पड़ता था। ऐसे में हम साल में २-४ गाड़ी मूंग, मूंगफली वगैरह

की मंगवा कर बेच देते थे। जो मुनाफा मिलता, उससे ये सब खर्चे चल जाते थे और कुछ बचत भी हो जाती थी ।

साझे में कारोबार

जोरहाट रहते हुए मुझे सात-आठ साल हो गए थे। काफी लोगों से पहचान हो गई थी। हमने १९५७-५८ में पदमाराम ओमप्रकाश (मारवाड़ी पट्टी) के यहां मूंग और हरदेवदास मदनलाल (एटी रोड टोकलाई ब्रिज) के यहां मूंगफली की बिल्टी लेनी शुरू की। इससे हमारी आर्थिक स्थिति काफी ठीक हुई। हमने जोरहाट में खुद का व्यापार करने का मानस बनाया। हालांकि इसके लिए दुकान और रकम का जुगाड़ नहीं था। मार्च १९५९ में मैं एक दिन हरदेवदास मदनलाल फर्म के सिंघी भाइयों (छगनलालजी सिंघी और मदनलालजी सिंघी) से मिला। उन्हें राजा मैदान रोड की दुकान भाड़े पर देने का अनुरोध किया। मैंने उन्हें बताया कि मैं बिजली और हार्डवेयर का छोटा-मोटा काम करने की सोच रहा हूं। सिंघी भाइयों से हमारा खास परिचय नहीं था। बानूड़ा में उनके रिश्तेदार रहते थे। वे हमारे परिवार को अच्छी तरह जानते थे। उन्होंने मुझसे कहा, आप कल आना। कल बात करेंगे। अगले दिन जब मैं उनके पास गया तो बोले, किराए पर दुकान नहीं दूंगा, पर हां पार्टनरशिप में

काम कर सकता हूं। मैंने कहा, आप हमारे बारे में पूरा पता कर लें। आपको तसल्ली हो जाये तो हम पार्टनरशिप में काम कर सकते हैं । लेकिन मेरे पास पैसे नहीं हैं। मैं केवल काम संभाल सकता हूं । उनको बिजली और हार्डवेयर का कोई अनुभव नहीं था। बिजली और हार्डवेयर की दुकानें भी उस समय दो-तीन ही थीं। वैसे भी भारत के पूर्वोत्तर राज्य बिजली के क्षेत्र में काफी पिछड़े हुए थे । हमने यहां की इस जरूरत को समझा और इसी दिशा में काम करने का फैसला लिया। इसके चलते इस काम में मुनाफा ज्यादा होने की उम्मीद थी । उन्होंने कहा, हमें आपके बारे में पूरी तसल्ली हो गई थी तभी हमने आपको पार्टनरशिप का प्रस्ताव दिया था । अब आप बताओ, काम कब से शुरू करें। मैंने कहा, मैं कल अपने मालिक इमनादत्तजी से बात करके एक-दो दिन में बता दूंगा ।

मैंने इमनादत्तजी को बताया कि मैं अपना धंधा शुरू करना चाहता हूं। आप मुझे सेवा - मुक्त कर दीजिए। उन्होंने कहा, यदि तुम अपना काम करना चाहते हो तो मुझे कोई आपत्ति नहीं है, परन्तु यदि दूसरी जगह नौकरी करोगे तो मुझे बुरा लगेगा। मैंने कहा, दूसरी जगह नौकरी करने का तो सवाल ही नहीं उठता। मैं आपके यहां ९ साल से काम कर रहा हूं। मुझे दूसरी जगह जाने की क्या जरूरत है। तब उन्होंने कहा कि मार्च खत्म हो गया है । आप हमारे यहां चार महीने रहकर इस साल के

DELIGATION TO FICCI FROM UPPER ASSAM CHAMBER OF COMMERCE, JORHAT IN THE YEAR 1ST MAY, 1976 AT DEL HI FROM LEFT : SRI RAMAVTAR AGARWALLA, SRI MURLIDHAR KHETAN, SRI RAMESHWARLAL AGARWALLA, SRI GOKULCHAND JAJU AND SRI JUGAL KISHORE AGARWALLA, SECRETARY, UACC

खाते-बही का काम पूरा करके, तलपट बना दीजिए। मैं आपको १५०० रुपए महीने के हिसाब से ६००० रुपये दे दूंगा । आप यह काम तीन महीने में भी कर लेंगे, तो भी डॉ. मुरलीधर खेतान आपको ६००० रुपए दूंगा । पर छुट्टी ४

महीने होने पर ही मंजूर करूंगा । आपसे जो एक महीना और काम कराएंगे, उसका भी आपको अलग से १५०० रुपए मिल जायगा । मैंने कहा, ठीक है, कोशिश करता हूं । कल से काम चालू कर दूंगा, आज मुझे थोड़ा बाहर जाना है। मैं मदनलालजी सिंघी के पास गया और कहा कि मैं आपके साथ सीर में काम कर लूंगा, लेकिन सितम्बर के महीने से चालू कर सकता हूं। मैं १ सितंबर को आ जाऊंगा । बात पक्की हो गई। मैंने अगले दिन से इमनादत्तजी का काम निपटाना शुरू कर दिया। काम तीन महीने में पूरा हो गया। पूरा हिसाब और तलपट बनाकर उनके हाथ में दे दिया। अब उन्होंने मुझे, जैसा कि पहले ही कह दिया था, एक महीने और रुक कर उस साल का बिक्री कर और आयकर का रिटर्न भरने को कहा । यह भी कहा कि पैसा आपको एक महीने का ज्यादा मिल जायगा। मैंने वह काम भी शुरू कर दिया, पर वह एक महीने में पूरा नहीं हो सका । इमनादत्तजी ने कहा कि आप उसे पूरा करके ही जाइए, आपको पैसा और मिल जाएगा । १५-२० दिन में जब सारा काम पूरा हो गया तब मैंने कहा, महीने के शेष दिन आपका ही काम करूंगा, पर पैसा नही लूंगा । उन्होंने कहा, अब आप १० दिन आराम करो, काम नहीं करना है। जरूरी होगा तो बता दूंगा ।

उसी दिन शाम ५ बजे इमनादत्तजी मेरे पास आए । बोले, मुझे आपसे कुछ बात करनी है। आओ, मेरे पास गद्दी पर बैठो। मैंने कहा, मैं आपके साथ गद्दी पर कैसे बैठ सकता हूं । वे बड़ी आत्मीयता से हठ करते हुए बोले, नहीं-नहीं आपको गद्दी पर ही बैठना है । यह हमारा आदेश है। मैंने नम्रता से कहा, आपका आदेश है तो कैसे इन्कार कर सकता हूं। और मैं उनके पास बैठ गया। उन्होंने पूछा, आप काम अकेले कर रहे हो या किसी के साथ। मैंने सच-सच बता दिया, हरदेवदास मदनलाल फर्म के सिंघी भाइयों के साथ काम कर रहा हूं। उन्होंने कहा, उनके साथ काम में मुझे कोई आपत्ति नहीं। है। पर आप मुझे पार्टनरशिप की डीड बताकर ही निर्णय लेंगे। मैंने कहा, ठीक है । १ सितम्बर १९५९ को मैं सिंघी भाइयों के यहां आ गया। हम लोग दुकान गये । उनके पास फर्नीचर कुछ तो था । जरूरत का और बनवाया । उन्होंने पार्टनरशिप की डीड भी बना रखी थी। हिस्से की बात न उन्होंने की, न मैंने। मैंने सोचा, उनको

ही बोलने देता हूं। लेकिन उन्होंने इतना ही पूछा कि पार्टनरशिप में आपकी तरफ से किस किसका नाम देना है। मैंने कहा, मेरा और मेरे भाई नेमीचन्द का । इसके अलावा कोई बात नहीं हुई । जब उन्होंने मुझे पार्टनरशिप डीड की कॉपी दी तब मालूम हुआ कि हमारा हिस्सा ४९ प्रतिशत और उनका ५१ प्रतिशत था। मैंने इस पर ज्यादा विचार नहीं किया। सोचा इससे कोई खास फर्क नहीं पड़ने वाला है। पार्टनरशिप डीड की कॉपी इमनादत्तजी को दिखाई, तो वे बोले, बाकी सब तो ठीक है, पर साझेदारी आधी-आधी होनी चाहिये। मैंने कहा, मुझे १ प्रतिशत में कोई फर्क नहीं पड़ेगा । काम शुरू कर पाऊं बस । उन्होंने कहा, ठीक है, और काम शुरू करिए। हमसे किसी तरह की कभी कोई सहायता चाहिए, तो निसंकोच बोल देना । हम आपके साथ हैं। मैंने अपना आभार प्रकट किया और आज्ञा लेकर आ गया ।

सिंघी भाइयों के साथ मैंने राजा मैदान में दुकान शुरू कर दी। नाम रखा-यूनाइटेड हार्डवेयर एंड इलेक्ट्रिकल स्टोर्स । मुहूर्त पूजन के बाद बिक्री का काम चालू हो गया। पूजन में शामिल हुए लोग जब चले गए तो छगनलालजी और मदनलालजी ने कहा कि मुरलीधरजी दुकान तो आपको ही चलानी है । हम लोग यहां नहीं बैठेंगे। मैंने कहा, कोई बात नहीं, आपको कोई शिकायत नहीं मिलेगी। दुकान पर एक-दो आदमी और रख लिए। २-३ दिन बाद में उन्होंने मुझसे कहा कि कलकत्ता से १५ हजार तक का माल लाना है। कलकत्ता में पांचीराम भोमसिंह की गद्दी ४६ स्ट्रेण्ड रोड पर दूसरी मंजिल पर थी । उस समय असम में ज्यादातर माल कलकत्ता से निमाती घाट पर जहाज के जरिए ही आता था। ट्रांसपोर्ट कंपनी एक-दो ही थी, इसलिए उसका किराया बहुत लगता था । इसकी अपेक्षा जहाज का भाड़ा कम था। इसलिए मैंने माल लेकर निमाती घाट के लिए जहाज बुक करवा लिया । सितबंर १९५९ से मार्च १९६० तक सात महीना काम किया । इस दौरान माल वगैरह लाने में कुल १ महीना लग गया। ऐसे में काम ६ महीने ही हुआ । माल गुवाहाटी से भी आता था। वहां भी पांचीराम भोमसिंह की गद्दी थी । ६ महीने के काम का हिसाब किया तो देखा कि बिक्री बहुत अच्छी हुई थी। मुनाफा भी कुल ७ लाख रुपए का। हमारे तीन लाख तयालीस हजार रुपए और उनके तीन लाख सत्तावन हजार हिस्से में

आए। दुकान अच्छी चलती देख दोनों भाई बोले, अब आप जितना माल लाना चाहो, ला सकते हैं। दो साल दुकान अच्छी चली, कमाई भी बढ़िया हुई ।

नामरूप में दो प्रोजेक्ट

१९६२ में सरकार ने नामरूप (डिब्रूगढ़, असम) में दो परियोजनाएं शुरू करने का निश्चय किया था । एक थर्मल का और दूसरा फर्टिलाइजर का । करोड़ों की लागत की ये परियोजनाएं जब शुरू हुईं तो हमने भी साइट पर झोंपड़ी बनवाकर डेरा डाल लिया । सुविधा के लिए एक सहायक रख लिया। वह खाना बना लेता था । हम पत्तल में खाते, सकोरे में चाय पीते । फिर उन्हें जंगल में फेंक आते थे। सरकार ने भी अपने कच्चे ऑफिस बनवा लिये थे और उसी में काम चालू कर दिया था । हम दिनभर वहीं रहते थे। वहीं माल का ऑर्डर निकलवा लेते और जोरहाट से लाकर दे देते । १९६२ में ही हमने बिरलाजी की एम्बेसडर कार खरीदी थी । बारह हजार पांच सौ रुपए में । मैं

डॉ. मुरलीधर खेतान

उसी कार से सोमवार को नामरूप जाता और शनिवार को वापस जोरहाट आ जाता। मेरा आदमी साइट पर ही रहता। दोनों परियोजनाओं में हमें अच्छा काम मिलने लगा । हमारी अच्छी साख बन गई थी । हमने १९६२ से १९६५ तक काफी अच्छा कारोबार किया ।

धंधे के बीच कभी-कभी ऐसे संकट आ जाते हैं कि आपको सब काम-धाम छोड़कर पहले उसे देखना होता है । और जब यह संकट अपनी संतान पर आता है, तो आप कुछ और नहीं सोच पाते हैं। ऐसा ही एक हादसा १९६९ में हुआ। मेरा दूसरा बेटा बसंत डेढ़ साल का था। मैं जब भी दुकान जाता, वह साथ चलने की जिद करने लगता। एक दिन जब मैं उसे अपने साथ दुकान ले गया, तो अचानक उसे अजीब-सी नींद और बेहोशी छाने लगी। वह अचेतन होने लगा। मेरे साथ मदन लाल सिंघी थे । उन्होंने कहा, 'लगता है, बच्चे की तबीयत ठीक नहीं है, आप इसे तुरंत अस्पताल ले जाएं।' मैं उसे मिशन हॉस्पिटल लेकर भागा, जो उस समय शहर का एक मात्र अच्छा अस्पताल था। डॉक्टर ने देखते ही कहा, अच्छा किया आप इसे वक्त पर ले आए। लगता है इसने कोई नशीली चीज खा ली है। घर पता किया, तो मालूम हुआ कि उसने मेरी पत्नी की नींद की दवा खा ली थी। उन दिनों मेरी पत्नी की तबीयत ठीक नहीं थी और वह दवा डॉक्टर ने ही उसे लिखी थी । ना जाने कैसे उसके हाथ

लग गई और वह खा गया। डॉक्टर ने बसंत का इलाज किया। होश आने में पूरे २४ घंटे लग गए। तब तक घर से सब आ गए थे । अस्पताल के बाहर उसके ठीक होने का इंतजार कर रहे थे । बसंत को होश आया तब सबके जी में जी आया ।

स्वतंत्र व्यवसाय

इस बीच डिब्रूगढ़ में नौकरी कर रहे मेरे छोटे भाई नेमीचन्द ने जोरहाट में ६ जून १९६४ से मोटर पार्ट्स का काम शुरू कर दिया था । बजरंगलाल सिंघी के साथ साझेदारी में। दुकान का नाम रखा अग्रवाल मोटर स्टोर्स । यहां भी काम ठीक चल रहा था । फिर १९७५ में नेमीचन्द ने खेतान मोटर्स नाम से अपनी अलग दुकान कर ली । वह आज भी है । १९८२ तक हम सब भाई साथ ही थे । १९७९ में यूनाइटेड हार्डवेयर एंड इलेक्ट्रिकल स्टोर्स की दुकान के खुडावण (माल के खरीद-फरोख्त की सूची) का हिसाब हो गया था । मैंने मदनलालजी से कहा, अब हम लोग अलग-अलग हो जाते हैं । मदनलालजी ने पूछा, आप अलग क्यों हो रहे हैं, क्या तकलीफ है ? हिस्सेदारी कम हो तो और ले लीजिए। मैंने कहा, हिस्सेदारी की तो बात ही नहीं है । २० सालों में मैंने कभी इसका सवाल नहीं उठाया। हमारा अलग-अलग होना इस समय दोनों के हित में है । अभी हम राजी - राजी अलग हो जाएंगे, किसी को पता भी नहीं चलेगा। बाद में कठिनाई होगी। तब उन्होंने कहा, यदि आप चाहते ही हैं तो ठीक है । आपको दुकान की गुडविल का कितना पैसा देना है। मैंने

कहा, मुझे गुडविल का एक भी पैसा नहीं चाहिए । जो पैसा खाते-बही में मेरे नाम से जमा है, वो ही दे दें । १ अप्रैल १९७९ को अलग होकर हमने ३१ मई १९७९ को सिंघी भाइयों की दुकान के पास ही दुकान खोल ली। दुकान का नाम रखा हाईटेंशन इलेक्ट्रिकल्स । आज भी जोरहाट में लोग इसी नाम से जानते हैं। हालांकि हमने हाईटेंशन बंद करके दूसरे नाम से काम कर लिया है। हाईटेंशन का काम बहुत अच्छा चल रहा था। बिजली विभाग में टेंडर भी मिलता और दुकानदारी भी ठीक थी। बड़ा बेटा जयप्रकाश भी काम में हाथ बंटाने लगा था । बसंत और प्रदीप उस समय पढ़ रहे थे। दुकान का काम पूरी रफ्तार पर था।

इंडस्ट्री में निवेश

१९८३ में असम राज्य विद्युत मंडल ने निर्णय लिया कि केबल और कंडक्टर का उत्पादन करने वाली इंडस्ट्री को ही टेंडर दिया जाएगा। ऐसे में हमारा इंडस्ट्री में निवेश करना जरूरी हो गया था । हमने लाइसेंस के लिए आवेदन दिया । यह हमें २७ दिसंबर १९८४ को मिल गया। लाइसेंस का नंबर था २२७५ । जोरहाट के इंडस्ट्रियल एस्टेट में जमीन लेकर फैक्ट्री का निर्माण शुरू करवा दिया । इस तरह १९८४ में निकोन पावर एंड इंफ्रा लिमिटेड के तौर पर कंपनी का निगमीकरण होने के बाद जोरहाट (असम) में केबल और कंडक्टर उत्पादन की हमारी पहली इकाई की शुरुआत हुई । फैक्ट्री यूनिट - १ का उद्घाटन ३० सितंबर १९८६ को हुआ । उद्घाटन की व्यवस्था नीरेन शर्मा के जिम्मे थी । वे हमारी बहू रंजना (जयप्रकाश की पत्नी) के मुंह बोले भाई हैं। घर के हर छोटे-बड़े काम में हाजिर रहते हैं । उद्घाटन के लिए नीरेन ने राज्य के तत्कालीन ऊर्जा मंत्री ललित राजखोवा, उद्योग मंत्री दिगेन बोड़ा और स्थानीय विधायक अभिजीत शर्मा को आमंत्रित किया। इस तरह ३० सितंबर १९८६ को हमारी फैक्ट्री में उत्पादन का काम चालू हो गया । और हमें असम राज्य विद्युत मंडल

से टेंडर मिलना शुरू हो गया। उसमें जो सबसे कम दर आती थी, उसमें ९ प्रतिशत मूल्य वरीयता जोड़कर ऑर्डर देते थे । हमें करीब १२ - १३ प्रतिशत नफा होता था। यह काम १९८९ तक चलता रहा । उस समय असम में तीन फैक्ट्रियां थीं। एक हमारी निकॉन, दूसरी पूर्वांचल केबल एंड कंडक्टर प्राइवेट लिमिटेड तथा तीसरी शांति केबल एंड कंडक्टर्स प्राइवेट लिमिटेड। ऑर्डर सबको

बराबर मिलता था। कोई झगड़ा वगैरह नहीं था । मैं एसीएमए (असम कंडक्टर्स मैन्युफैक्चरर्स एसोसिएशन) का सचिव था और पीसीसी के रामगोपालजी अग्रवाल उस समय एसीएमए के अध्यक्ष थे ।

३१ मार्च १९८९ को असम सरकार ने स्थानीय फैक्ट्रियों को प्रोत्साहित करने के लिए एक नया कानून बना दिया । स्थानीय इंडस्ट्री को १५ प्रतिशत मूल्य वरीयता मिलनी चाहिए और बाहर की किसी भी पार्टी को ऑर्डर नहीं मिलेगा । इस अधिनियम का नाम एपीएसपी एक्ट (असम प्रीफरेंशियल स्टोर्स परचेज एक्ट) था । असम सरकार ने माल की रेट तय करने के लिए एक तीन सदस्यीय समिति बनाई । उसमें उद्योग विभाग के निदेशक, असम राज्य विद्युत मंडल के अध्यक्ष और असम केबल्स एंड कंडक्टर्स के सचिव थे। ये तीनों रेट तय करते । रेट तय करने का फार्मूला था- रॉ मेटीरियल्स इंक्लूडिंग आउटसाइड सीएसटी तथा माल उतारने का खर्च और माल भाड़ा, दो महीने का ब्याज (जब तक माल आकर माल बनकर तैयार हो जाता), और १५ प्रतिशत मुनाफा । उनसे मेरी अच्छी जानकारी थी। जब तक रेट तय नहीं हुई थी, ऑर्डर पूर्व रेट पर ही मिलता ।

उसमें यह शर्त थी कि अगर समिति की रेट ज्यादा हुई, तो माल देने वाले को रेट का अंतर अलग से ऑर्डर देकर दिया जाय। और अगर रेट कम होती है तो डिफ्रेंस की कीमत वापस की जाय । ३० जुलाई १९८९ को रेट

फाइनल हो गई। रेट ठीक ही हुई थी । १ अगस्त १९८९ से नई रेट से ऑर्डर होने लगे । पुराने ऑर्डर में संशोधन कर दिया गया। एसीएसआर (ऐलुमिनियम कंडक्टर स्टील - रिइन्फोर्ड केबल) का काम १९९३ तक चलता रहा । १९९३ के बाद सरकार ने निर्णय लिया कि अब एसीएसआर की जगह एएएसी (ऑल ऐलुमिनियम अलॉय कंडक्टर्स) खरीदने हैं । १ जून १९९३ में एएएसी की रेट फिर से पहले वाले फार्मूला पर तय की गई। इस बीच एक और इंडस्ट्री सिंघी केबल्स एंड कंडक्टर्स प्राइवेट लिमिटेड शुरू हो गई । अब तीन की जगह चार ऑर्डर होने लगे ।

१९९८ तक काम अच्छे-से चलता रहा । १९९८ के बाद माल देने वाली फैक्ट्रियों में मनमुटाव रहने लगा। काम में तरह-तरह की बाधाएं आने लगीं। इस बीच एक पार्टी ने कोर्ट में केस भी कर दिया था। इन हालात में असम राज्य विद्युत मंडल ने एपीएसपी एक्ट को खत्म करके माल फिर से टेंडर पर लेने का फैसला किया। टेंडर बाहर भी भेजा जाय और जिसकी रेट 'एल१' है, उसी को ऑर्डर दिया जाए। इस लड़ाई-झगड़े में २ साल चले गये। फिर असम

राज्य विद्युत मंडल ने सारा काम 'टर्नकी' पर कर दिया। इसके तहत जिसे ठेका दिया जाएगा, वही काम करेगा। सामान और श्रम सब कुछ उसका होगा । असम राज्य विद्युत मंडल को लाइन या सबस्टेशन का काम देखना होता था। नियमों के हिसाब से और टेंडर में दी गई शर्तों के हिसाब से भी । यह काम

भी असम राज्य विद्युत मंडल टेंडर देकर ही करता था । हमारे लिए काम नया था । हमने यह काम पहले नहीं किया था। इसका कोई अनुभव नहीं था । हमारे पास और कोई काम नहीं था। फैक्ट्री बंद हो चुकी थी । हमने मिल बैठकर कॉन्ट्रेक्ट पर काम शुरू करना तय किया। इस तरह 'टर्नकी' पर काम शुरू हुआ। शुरू में थोड़ी दिक्कतें आईं। फिर काम अच्छा चलने लगा और आज तक चल रहा है। उसका सारा श्रेय मेरे बड़े बेटे जयप्रकाश को जाता है । 'टर्नकी' का सारा काम उसी की निगरानी में हुआ था ।

राजस्थान में कारोबार

National Award by President of India Shri K.R. Narayanan New Delhi.

जोरहाट में कंडक्टर्स की फैक्ट्री के बाद केबल्स की फैक्ट्री की भी आवश्यकता महसूस हुई। हमने यूनिट नॉर्थ ईस्ट केबल्स प्राइवेट लिमिटेड के नाम से १९८९ में फैक्ट्री के निर्माण का काम शुरू किया। उत्पादन फरवरी १९९० में शुरू हुआ। यहां पावर केबल, अंडरग्राउंड केबल्स. ११ केवी तक के हाईटेंशन केबल्स बनते हैं। फैक्ट्री का काम पहले तो बहुत चला। बाद में जब असम राज्य विद्युत मंडल ने एपीएसपी एक्ट खत्म कर दिया तब काम कम होने लगा। जोरहाट की कंडक्टर फैक्ट्री से मांग पूरी नहीं हो पा रही थी इसलिए हमने एक और फैक्ट्री लगाना तय किया। इस बार जोरहाट से बाहर चाहते थे। हम सब की इच्छा राजस्थान में फैक्ट्री लगाने की थी। अपनी जन्मभूमि सीकर में । १९९० में मैं और जयप्रकाश सीकर आ गए। जोरहाट का काम बसंत देखता रहा। हमने सीकर में किराए का मकान लिया । जब एक साल में अपना घर बन गया, तो उसमें चले गए। साथ ही फैक्ट्री निर्माण का काम भी चलता रहा।

फैक्ट्री में कंडक्टर्स बनाने का काम २४ दिसंबर १९९१ में शुरू हुआ। यह थी निकोन पावर एंड इंफ्रा लिमिटेड की हमारी दूसरी इकाई, फैक्ट्री यूनिट - २ ।

पर राजस्थान की रेट और माहौल हमारे अनुकूल नहीं थे। फैक्ट्री दो साल बंद रही। १९९२ में प्रदीप ने बीईई कर लिया था। सीकर की फैक्ट्री का काम उसे सौंप कर सारी बातें समझा दीं। मैं भी साथ रहा। कुछ दिन जयप्रकाश भी। फैक्ट्री और मकान जयप्रकाश की देखरेख में ही बने थे। बहुत मेहनत हुई थी ।

उस समय भैरोंसिंहजी शेखावत राजस्थान के मुख्यमंत्री थे । वे मेरे गुरु भी रहे थे। फैक्ट्री से संबंधित काम के लिए हम उनके पास कई बार गये। हम उन्हें जो भी कागज देते, वे उस पर नोट डालकर राजस्थान राज्य विद्युत मंडल को भेज देते थे । यह क्रम १२ महीने तक चलता रहा। पर हमें सफलता नहीं मिली। एक दिन अचानक राजस्थान राज्य विद्युत मंडल के अध्यक्ष के पीए का फोन आया कि आपकी कंपनी के सीएमडी से हमारे चेयरमैन साहब जयपुर में मिलना चाहते हैं । हमने कहा कल ११ बजे का समय रख लीजिए। तब उन्होंने साहब से पूछकर हमें वापस सूचित किया कि हम उनसे ११ बजे मिल सकते हैं। मैं और प्रदीप दोनों पौने ग्यारह बजे ही मंडल के गेस्ट हाउस पहुंच गये और अपना विजिटिंग कार्ड उनको भेज दिया । ठीक ११ बजे उन्होंने हमें बुला लिया। हम उन्हें नमस्कार करके खड़े रहे । अध्यक्ष महोदय ने हमें सामने बैठने का इशारा किया। हम बैठ गये । वे वोले, आप १२ महीने से हमारे ऑफिस और सीएम साहब के चक्कर लगा रहे हैं। उन्होंने पत्रों का एक बंडल दिखाते

हुए कहा, आपने जितनी भी चिट्ठियां सीएम साहब को भेजीं, वे सब साइन होकर हमारे पास आ गई थीं । अब बोलिए, आप क्या चाहते हैं। हमने कहा,

साहब हमने नई फैक्ट्री लगाई है। हमें कुछ सुविधा मिल जाती। उन्होंने कहा, आप असम से राजस्थान आये हैं। असम और राजस्थान के माहौल में बहुत अंतर है। हम यहां नई-पुरानी किसी भी फैक्ट्री को सब्सीडी नहीं देते हैं । आपको हमारी निर्धारित रेट पर ही काम करना होगा। आप एक साल से कोशिश कर

National Award by Prime Minister of India
Dr. Manmohan Singh New Delhi.

रहे हैं । इसलिए हम इतना जरूर कर सकते हैं कि आप जितना चाहें उतनी मात्रा का ऑर्डर ले सकते हैं । रेट हमारी ही होगी, देख लीजिए। आप कितना माल भेजेंगे, यह बता दीजिए। ऑर्डर आज ही चला जाएगा। लेकिन जितने माल का ऑर्डर एक बार चला जाएगा, उसे आपको पूरा करना पड़ेगा । हमने हाथों हाथ एक कागज पर एसीएसआर वीजल १०००० किमी, एसीएसआर डॉग ५००० किमी और माल भेजने की तिथि लिख दी। इस बीच चाय-पानी चलता रहा। हमारा कागज देखकर वे बहुत खुश हुए और बोले आपके पास आज ही ऑर्डर पहुंच जाएगा। चेयरमैन साहब का नाम पी. एन. भंडारी था । हम वहां से गांव गए । खाना खाकर तुरंत सीकर आए। शाम करीब ६ बजे पहुंचते ही देखा कि ऑफिस में ऑर्डर का तार पड़ा हुआ है। उसमें ' ऑर्डर फोलो' लिखकर माल की मात्रा लिखी हुई थी । हमने जी जान लगाकर निश्चित तिथि पर माल भेज दिया। हमें समय पर उसका पैसा भी मिल गया।

शुरुआत में सीकर की फैक्ट्री में राजस्थान के ही मजदूर थे । यहां १२-१२ घंटे की दो शिफ्ट हैं। सुबह ८ से रात ८ तक और रात ८ से सुबह ८ तक। काम खत्म होते ही मजदूर अपने-अपने गांव चले जाते थे । यह कह कर कि कल सुबह वापस आ जाएंगे। लेकिन घर जाकर फोन कर देते, 'म्हारो काको

बीमार होगो, आज कोनी आ सकूं।' उनके नहीं आने से फैक्ट्री के काम में बाधा पड़ती थी। माल तो निश्चित तारीख पर भेजना ही होता था । हमें काफी तकलीफ होती थी । आखिर असम से मजदूर लाने पड़े। कुछ हमारी फैक्ट्री से और कुछ दूसरे । ३० के करीब मजदूर । राजस्थान में ये २०-२५ साल से हैं। अच्छा काम कर रहे हैं। राजस्थान के ५० डिग्री तापमान में भी काम कर लेते हैं, तो ० डिग्री तापमान में भी । उनके रहने-खाने की व्यवस्था फैक्ट्री में ही की हुई है इसलिए उन्हें फैक्ट्री से बाहर जाने की जरूरत नहीं पड़ती। इससे हमें भी काम करवाने में आसानी हुई। वे अपने घर असम बारी-बारी से जाते हैं । ३-४ आदमी हम ज्यादा ही रखते हैं, ताकि काम में कोई रुकावट नहीं हो ।

अब तक हमारी साख असम के अलावा राजस्थान, उत्तरप्रदेश, मध्यप्रदेश में अच्छी हो गई थी । काम अच्छा मिलने लगा। पर हम सीकर की फैक्ट्री से आपूर्ति पूरी नहीं कर पा रहे थे । जोरहाट से मंगवाते तो कच्चा माल भेजने और वहां से तैयार माल आने का भाड़ा बहुत ज्यादा लग जाता ।

इसलिए हमने जयपुर के आसपास एक और फैक्ट्री लगाने का विचार किया। राजस्थान राज्य विद्युत मंडल का ऑफिस भी जयपुर ही था । सारा काम यहीं से होना था। पहले जयपुर में जमीनें देखीं। बहुत महंगी थीं। फिर हमें दौसा जिले के बापी गांव में वाजिब दामों पर मिल गई । २००९ में फैक्ट्री का निर्माण शुरू किया । १० नवंबर २०१० से माल बनने लगा । यह थी हमारी कंपनी की तीसरी निर्माण इकाई, फैक्ट्री यूनिट - ३ । दूसरी फैक्ट्री तक निर्माण की सालाना क्षमता १५,९०० एमटी थी। बापी के बाद से क्षमता २९००० एमटी प्रतिवर्ष हो गई। दौसा की फैक्ट्री अब भी चालू है । राजस्थान का टर्नओवर

१२० से १५० करोड़ सालाना होना शुरू हो गया । दूसरी ओर जोरहाट में हमने २००५ से 'टर्नकी' पर नया काम शुरू किया था। जयप्रकाश की मेहनत और लगन से आज भी चालू है । यह काम अच्छा चला। अच्छी कमाई हुई। बाद में असम राज्य विद्युत मंडल में काम कुछ कम हो गया, तो हमने २०१६ में पावर ग्रिड कारपोरेशन ऑफ इंडिया लिमिटेड (पीजीसीआईएल) का 'टर्नकी' का काम शुरू किया। वह आज भी चल रहा है ।

पावर सेक्टर में खुद को मजबूत बनाए रखने के लिए हमने २०१० में अकल (जैसलमेर) में विंड एनर्जी पर आधारित पावर प्लांट लगाया । इसकी बिजली पैदा करने की क्षमता १.५ एमडब्ल्यू है। प्लांट का उद्घाटन इसी साल २५ सितंबर को जोधपुर के कलेक्टर साहब ने किया था । यह अब भी चल रहा है ।

मेरा प्रकृति से बचपन से ही लगाव रहा है। सन् २०१२ की बात है कि मेरे छोटे पुत्र प्रदीप ने मुझे बताया कि भारत की सबसे बड़ी मानव निर्मित झील में एक टापू का टुकड़ा संयुक्त रूप से बिकाऊ है और यह बताया गया कि ९० स्कवायर किलोमीटर झील में काफी वन्य जीव जैसे की मगरमच्छ जंगली जानवर व भिन्न भिन्न प्रकार के प्रवासी पक्षीयों का आना जाना लगा रहता है ।

मैंने इस टापू के टुकडे को खरीदने की स्वीकृति दे दी जो कि राजस्थान के उदयपुर जिले के जयसमंद झील में भटवाड़ा टापू पर स्थित है आगे चलकर हमने इस पर एक आराम गाह बनवाया जो कि आजकल पेइंग गेस्ट हाऊस के रूप में चल रहा है ।

काफी सालो तक बिजली से सम्बन्धित कार्य करने के बाद मैने परिवार के सभी सदस्यों से चर्चा करके कृषि सम्बन्धि कार्य करने की सलाह दी जिसके तहत हमने एक संयुक्त प्रोजेक्ट ग्रीनटेक मेगा फूड पार्क की स्थापना राजस्थान में की। मेरे पौत्र श्रेष्ठ जो की अमेरिका में पढ़ाई करता था, उसके भारत आने पर मैने उसको फूड से सम्बन्धित कार्य करने की सलाह दी, हमने सन् २०२० में एक कम्पनी नोर्दन सोलवेन्टस (प्रा. लि.) के नाम से अजमेर जिले के रूपनगढ़ गाँव में स्थापना की जो कि मसालों से सम्बन्धित प्रदार्थो का उत्पादन करेगा। यह ईकाई मार्च सन् २०२२ तक उत्पादन में आ जायेगी ।

मेरे पौत्र श्रेष्ठ ने एक कम्पनी UniRely.com की स्थापना सन् २०१८ में की जिसमें वह भारत से इच्छुक विद्यार्थी को भारत से अमेरिका, कनाड़ा, सिंगापुर तथा अन्य देशों में आगे की पढ़ाई के लिए भेजता है । इस कम्पनी का सारा काम मेरे पौत्र श्रेष्ठ के अलावा मेरी पौत्र वधु सृष्टि तथा मेरा दुसरा पौत्र विशेष देखते हैं ।

उत्तरप्रदेश का वर्ल्ड बैंक टेंडर

१९९८ में उत्तरप्रदेश राज्य विद्युत मंडल (यूपीएसईबी) से वर्ल्ड बैंक का एक टेंडर निकला था । शर्त यह थी कि जिसके पास एसीएसआर वीजल कंडक्टर १५००० किमी या डॉग, अथवा दोनों की आपूर्ति का बिजली विभाग से प्रमाण-पत्र है, वही इस टेंडर को भर सकता है । केवल हमारे पास इसका सर्टिफिकेट था

National Award by Vice President of India Shri Krishankant New Delhi.

। और किसी पार्टी के पास नहीं था । हमने मिल बैठ कर विचार किया कि टेंडर बड़ा है और रेट निर्धारित की हुई है । पता नहीं दे या नहीं। मैंने कहा, धंधा करेंगे तो नफा-नुकसान दोनों उठाना पड़ेगा । किसी ने सही ही कहा है, 'जिसमें नुकसान सहने की ताकत हो, वही मुनाफा कमा सकता है । फिर वह कारोबार हो चाहे रिश्ता । ' हमें टेंडर भर देना चाहिए। सहमति बन गई, तो यूपीएसईबी से टेंडर पेपर मंगवाकर भर दिया। हमें बाद में मालूम हुआ कि केवल हमारा ही टेंडर गया था । चिन्ता हुई कि एक टेंडर पर विचार करेंगे या नहीं। तभी यूपीएसईबी से टेंडर की तारीख आगे खिसकने की सूचना मिली। साथ ही यह भी कि एक टेंडर होगा तब भी विचार कर लिया जाएगा। कारण यह था कि पैसे वर्ल्ड बैंक के थे । न लेते तो वापस चले जाते। टेंडर ३००० किमी एसीएसआर डॉग का था। उसमें हमें इंपोर्ट लाइसेंस भी मिलना था। इससे हम माल दूसरे देश से भी मंगवा सकते थे । हमने टेंडर भेज दिया । रेट भी

थोड़ी ज्यादा दे दी, यह जानकर कि टेंडर तो हमें मिलना ही है । खरीदार की अनुमानित कीमत तो टेंडर में आती ही है, उससे १० प्रतिशत ज्यादा तक विभाग में भेज सकते हैं । हमने ८ प्रतिशत ज्यादा रेट देकर, जरूरत के सभी कागज संलग्न करके फॉर्म भेज दिया । तकदीर ने साथ दिया और हमें ऑर्डर मिल गया। ऑर्डर के साथ ही इंपोर्ट लाइसेंस भी आ गया । हमारी मेहनत सफल हुई। थोड़ी चाह, थोड़ी कोशिश, थोड़ी मेहनत, थोड़ी उम्मीद। इन सबका दामन हम थामे रहे, तो मुकद्दर ने भी हमारा साथ दिया । और पूरा दिया । रेट निर्धारित थी । हमें कम-ज्यादा मिल नहीं सकती थी । किन्तु टेंडर आने के बाद बाजार में कच्चे माल के दाम काफी कम हो गए थे। और उधर डॉलर का दाम बढ़ता गया। हमारा ऑर्डर अमरीकी डॉलर में था । इससे दुगुना फायदा हुआ। अच्छा खासा मुनाफा हुआ। ३००० किमी का सिंगल ऑर्डर हाथ में रह गया था, जो बाद में काम आया ।

शुरूआती दौर

हमने 'टर्नकी' का काम लोअर असम से लेकर अपर असम तक किया। यहां भी मजदूरों की समस्या रहती थी । असम राज्य विद्युत मंडल का काम सिर्फ असम में ही होता था। अब हमने पावर ग्रिड का काम लिया। उसका काम असम के अलावा अरुणाचल, मेघालय में भी होता है। यहां भी हमें सन् २००८ - राष्ट्रीय पुरस्कार मजदूरों को लेकर बहुत दिक्कतें हैं । बाहर से लाकर काम चलाते हैं। पावर ग्रिड का काम थोड़ा कठिन है । उसमें बहुत

सारे परीक्षण करने होते हैं। यहां तक कि मिट्टी, बालू रेत, पत्थर, ईंट, सीमेंट आदि की भी जांच होती है । जांच भी हम ही करवाते हैं । फिर काम में लेते हैं। मैंने १९७४ से १९८५ तक नागालैंड, मणिपुर, मिजोरम में भी काम किया । नागालैंड में रात को ठहरने की जगह नहीं थी। नागालैंड की राजधानी कोहिमा में भी होटल नहीं थे । सिर्फ १-२ सरकारी गेस्ट हाउस थे । वहां कभी रुक जाते तो स्थानीय लोग हमें बाहर निकाल देते

थे। रात बरामदे में बितानी पड़ती थी । कोहिमा के बिजली विभाग का चीफ इंजीनियर मिस्टर टॉय बहुत ही भला था । एक दिन हमने उनसे कहा कि साहब रात को यहां ठहरने की कोई जगह नहीं है। बहुत तकलीफ होती है । तब उन्होंने अपने विभाग के गेस्ट हाउस में एक कमरे का स्थाई इंतजाम करवा दिया। अब जब भी कोहिमा जाते हैं, वहीं रुकते हैं ।

मैं और मेरे मित्र भोमराज प्रजापत एक ही कार में नागालैंड और कोहिमा जाते थे। हम एक ही काम करते थे, पर कभी मनमुटाव नहीं हुआ । हम लोग दाल, चावल, आटा साथ रखते थे । सब्जी बाजार से ले लेते थे । गेस्ट हाउस के कमरे में दो बैड थे । उन पर सो जाते । खाना गेस्ट हाउस का नेपाली चौकीदार बना देता था । हमें कोहिमा बिजली विभाग के चीफ इंजीनियर से ऑर्डर मिलता था । उनका सेंट्रल स्टोर दीमापुर था । इसलिए हम माल वहीं भेजते थे और भुगतान भी वहीं से होता था ।

एक बार जोरहाट से जुगल किशोर सिंघी, पूनमचन्द बोथरा तथा दीमापुर से आसोपाजी मणिपुर इम्फाल देखने मेरे साथ हो लिए । इम्फाल जब भी काम से अकेला जाता था, हमारे गांव के मदनलाल छाबड़ा के यहां रुकता था। लेकिन उस दिन हम चार आदमी थे । इसलिए गुवाहाटी होटल में रुकना पड़ा। होटल भी ऐसा मिला जिसमें पैसे वाले ताश खेलने आया करते थे। हमें ताश खेलने का बहुत शौक था । जोरहाट में हम लोग १९७५ से ही

Felicitated by Chief Minister of
Assam Shri Tarun Gogoi Guwahati.

रोजाना शाम पांच से साढ़े सात बजे तक ताश खेलते थे। कई साथी रहे उस दौर में। इनमें पूनमचन्द बोथरा, इंदरचंद बोथरा, गणेशमल बजाज, डॉक्टर शिवरतन

माहेश्वरी, रामावतार अग्रवाल, देवेंद्र शर्मा, महावीर चांडक, मन्नालाल कुंडलिया, बसंत बगड़िया, गोपीकिशन जाजू, पूरणमल सिंघी, देवीदत्त सिंघी, जगदीश अग्रवाल, राजकुमार सिंघी, शिव बाहेती, अवनि शर्मा, संतकुमार भूपाल, डॉक्टर शिवभगवान अग्रवाल, अर्जुनलाल केजड़ीवाल, रमेश शील, प्रहलाद पोद्दार, तनसुखजी पंडित, बिमल लोहिया, मदन गट्टाणी, भगवती प्रसाद गोयल जैसे कई नाम हैं । इनमें से कई अब इस दुनिया में नहीं हैं, लेकिन ताश की महफिल में उनकी यादें आज भी ताजा हैं। हम ताश केवल विशुद्ध मनोरंजन के लिए खेलते थे। दांव नहीं लगाते थे। हाईटेंशन इलेक्ट्रिकल्स दुकान के ऊपर कमरे में ताश चलती और हॉल में चौपड़ । दो ग्रुप होते । ताश के रसिकों की भीड़ लग जाती । चौपड़ खेलने वाले अब नहीं रहे । ताश अभी भी मनोरंजन का जरिया है। तो इम्फाल होटल में हम चारों ने ताश खेलना शुरू किया। तभी एक पुलिस वाला वहां आ गया। थोड़ी देर खड़ा रहा। फिर उसे तसल्ली हो गई कि हम कोई दांव नहीं लगा रहे हैं, तो चला गया ।

ताश की बात चली है, तो मुझे मेरे जीवन की एक अत्यंत दुखद घटना याद आ रही है। तारीख थी २९ अगस्त और साल १९९८ । जीवन का कोई भरोसा नहीं है। पता नहीं कब क्या हो जाए। कुछ ऐसा ही मेरे भाई नेमीचंद के साथ हुआ। एक दिन मैं दोस्तों के साथ ताश खेल रहा था । नेमीचंद भी साथ ही था । वह भी खेल रहा था। ताश खेलते-खेलते अचानक उसके सीने में तेज दर्द उठा। उस दिन हम दस-बारह दोस्त खेल रहे थे। उनमें दो डॉक्टर भी थे। डॉक्टर ने कुछ दवाइयां दीं, पर वह बुरी तरह छटपटाने लगा। पीड़ा में वह केवल मेरे बड़े बेटे जय प्रकाश का नाम ले रहा था। उसे तुरंत बुलाया । नेमीचंद ने आखिरी बार प्रकाश कहा और देखते ही देखते शांत हो गया। उसके प्राण पखेरु उड़ गए। सब घर पर थे । उन्हें सूचना दी। इंसान के जीवन का सच में कोई पता नहीं चलता, अभी है और अगले पल नहीं । नेमीचंद अच्छा भला था । उम्र भी सिर्फ ६१ थी। किसको पता था कि अचानक यह सब हो जाएगा।

अब मैं वापस इम्फाल पर आता हूं। दूसरे दिन हम लोग इम्फाल में थोड़ा घूम-फिर कर वापस दीमापुर आ गये । दीमापुर में हमने किराए से एक कमरा ले रखा था। उसी में सब सो गये। अगले दिन दीमापुर में थोड़ा काम था, उसे

किया और शाम को वापस जोरहाट आ गए। वैसे नागालैंड और मणिपुर में हमने काफी काम किया है। जयप्रकाश और मैं दोनों ही वहां का काम देखते थे। नागालैंड में मोकोकचुंग में जेठमल सुथार के साथ हमारी मोटर पार्ट्स की दुकान थी। छोटे भाई नेमीचन्द के साले गिरधारीजी हमारी तरफ से उसमें साझेदार थे। हफ्ता दस दिन से नेमीचन्द भी मोकोकचुंग जाता था। मै तो बराबर जाता ही था। वहां के बिजली विभाग से ऑर्डर लेता, उन्हें माल देता और भुगतान लेता। एक बार गाड़ी से जाते समय नेमीचन्द का एक्सीडेंट हो गया। रात में फोन से मालूम हुआ, तो मैं और जुगल किशोर मोकोकचुंग भागे । नेमीचन्द को जोरहाट लाकर दिखाया। हाथ में फ्रैक्चर हो गया था। एक महीने का प्लास्टर बंधा । वह ठीक हुआ तब जी में जी आया ।

वर्तमान में निकोन

हमने हमारी कंपनी निकोन पावर एंड इंफ्रा लिमिटेड को दिसंबर १९८४ में विधिवत रजिस्टर करवाया था। तब से ही देश के पावर सेक्टर में हमारा खास योगदान रहा है। खासकर पूर्वोत्तर क्षेत्रों में। पहले हम नार्थ ईस्टर्न केबल्स एंड कंडक्टर्स प्राइवेट लिमिटेड के नाम से काम कर रहे थे ।

National Award by Minister of
MSME Shri Kalraj Misra New Delhi.

जिस समय मैं जोरहाट आया था, असम बिजली के क्षेत्र में काफी पिछड़ा हुआ था। वहां की जरूरत को देखते हुए ही मैं इलेक्ट्रिकल व्यवसाय में आया। मुझे इसकी समझ भी थी। जैसा कि मैंने पहले भी कहा है, हमने सबसे पहले जोरहाट में ओवरहैड कंडक्टर्स बनाने की फैक्ट्री लगाई थी । वर्ष १९८६ में । यहां हमें अच्छी सफलता मिली। जोरहाट के बाद १९९१ में दूसरी फैक्ट्री सीकर (राजस्थान) में और तीसरी २०१० में बापी (दौसा, राजस्थान) में लगाई । दूसरी

फैक्ट्री तक निर्माण की सालाना क्षमता १५,९०० एमटी थी । तीसरी यूनिट की स्थापना के बाद २९,००० एमटी प्रतिवर्ष हो गई । हम अपने उत्पाद की गुणवत्ता बनाए रखने के लिए कच्चे माल की समय-समय पर समीक्षा करते रहते हैं । अच्छा माल कहां से मिल सकता है, इस पर विचार करते हैं । हमारे इलेक्ट्रिकल उत्पाद समय पर बन जाएं, ऑर्डर के हिसाब से उनकी आपूर्ति तय समय पर हो सके, इसका हम विशेष ध्यान रखते हैं । हम ८०० केवी एचवीडीसी कंडक्टर्स सहित ११ केवी से ७६५ केवी तक के एएएसी, एएसी, एसीएसआर ओवरहैड कंडक्टर्स बनाते हैं । इनका उपयोग पावर ट्रांसमिशन और डिस्ट्रिब्यूशन लाइंस के निर्माण में होता है । हम ग्राउंड वायर्स और जीआई वायर्स भी बनाते हैं। बाद में हम पावर के अलावा इंफ्रास्ट्रक्चर और पाइपलाइंस के क्षेत्र में भी आ गए।

ओवरहैड कंडक्टर्स बनाने के लिए हम सबसे पहले इलेक्ट्रोलिटिक प्रोसेस से एल्युमिनियम को शोधित करते हैं । इस प्रक्रिया में परिष्कृत एल्युमिनियम ९९.५ प्रतिशत रह जाता है । हमारे कंडक्टर्स में जंग नहीं लगती। मजबूत होने के कारण खिंच कर टूटते नहीं हैं । इन खूबियों के कारण ही ओवरहैड कंडक्टर्स का उपयोग ओवरहैड ट्रांसमिशन और डिस्ट्रिब्यूशन लाइंस में होता है। कंडक्टर्स के विभिन्न उपयोगों के कारण ही इनको समान्यतया पावर ट्रांसमिशन और डिस्ट्रिब्यूशन सेक्टर में काम में लेते हैं। ओवरहैड कंडक्टर्स के सभी प्रकारों का शहरी और ग्रामीण क्षेत्रों में पावर ट्रांसमिशन और डिस्ट्रिब्यूशन लाइंस बनाने के लिए व्यापक रूप से होता है। ये कंडक्टर्स एल्युमिनियम तारों के एक से ज्यादा स्ट्रेंड (तार) के बने होते हैं और जरूरत के हिसाब से ६१ स्ट्रेंड्स तक के बन सकते हैं । इनकी अधिष्ठापित क्षमता ५०,००० एमटी प्रतिवर्ष है । इन पर औद्योगिक मानदंडों के हिसाब से आईएसआई मार्क है । गुणवत्ता प्रबंधन प्रणाली के लिए आईएसओ ९००१ : २०१५ प्राप्त है । हम अब तक ट्रांसमिशन के लिए ३८,८३९ किमी और डिस्ट्रिब्यूशन के लिए १०३, ४८७ किमी ओवरहैड कंडक्टर्स बना चुके हैं ।

पिछले कुछ वर्षों से हम ईपीसी (इंजीनियरिंग, प्रोक्योरमेंट एंड कंस्ट्रक्शन) कांट्रेक्ट्स और 'टर्नकी' प्रोजेक्ट्स का उपयोग कर रहे हैं। हमने ४०० केवी, २२० केवी, १३२ केवी, ३३केवी, ११केवी सब-स्टेशंस, ट्रांसमिशन और डिस्ट्रिब्यूशन लाइंस की आपूर्ति की है । सरकार ने पावर डिस्ट्रिब्यूशन सेक्टर को विकसित करने के

लिए कई योजनाएं शुरू की थीं। खासकर भारत के पूर्वोत्तर में । असम पावर सेक्टर इंवेस्टमेंट प्रोग्राम (एशियन डवलपमेंट बैंक ने इसका पैसा दिया था), दीनदयाल उपाध्याय ग्राम ज्योति योजना, इंटीग्रेटिड पावर डवलपमेंट स्कीम, राजीव गांधी ग्रामीण विद्युतिकरण योजना, ट्रेड डवलपमेंट फंड स्कीम, असम बिकास योजना, नार्थ ईस्टर्न पावर सिस्टम इंप्रूवमेंट प्रोजेक्ट जैसी योजनाओं के लिए हमने आपूर्ति की है ।

हम आठ साल से ज्यादा समय से पावर ग्रिड कारपोरेशन ऑफ इंडिया लिमिटेड (पीजीसीआईएल) को अपना माल सप्लाई कर रहे हैं, जिसमें कभी कोई शिकायत नहीं आई है। हम उनके ७६५ केवी / ८०० केवी एचवीडीसी कंडक्टर्स के ऑर्डर सफलतापूर्वक पूरे कर चुके हैं। भारत में पावर ट्रांसमिशन और डिस्ट्रिब्यूशन सेक्टर में पीजीसीआईएल के लिए भी हमने ईपीसी / टर्नकी प्रोजेक्ट्स का उपयोग किया है । और कई स्टेट पावर यूटिलिटीज के लिए भी । पीजीसीआईएल देश की सबसे बड़ी ट्रांसमिशन यूटिलिटी है (स्रोत: आईसीआरए रिपोर्ट, सितंबर २०१८) हम उन्हें अच्छी गुणवत्ता वाले सभी प्रकार के ओवरहैड लाइंस की आपूर्ति करते हैं। पीजीसीआईएल हमारा सबसे बड़ा खरीदार है । २०१० में हमें पहला सबसे बड़ा ऑर्डर ओवरहैड लाइंस की आपूर्ति के लिए करीब ६८७ मिलियन रुपयों का मिला था ।

हमारा एक और अहम प्रोजेक्ट है बिजली जनरेट करना । जैसा कि मैंने पहले भी जिक्र किया है कि हमने २०१० में अकल (जैसलमेर) में विंड एनर्जी पर आधारित पावर प्लांट लगाया था। इसकी बिजली पैदा करने की क्षमता १.५ एमडब्ल्यू है ।

सन् २०१२ जैसलमेर हमने नदियों और जलाशयों आदि का पानी गांवों में घर-घर पहुंचाने के लिए अत्याधुनिक डीएल, जीएल पाइपलाइंस लगवाई हैं। इससे लोगों सन् २०२० ऑडिशा सन् २०२० ओडिशा को पीने का पानी आसानी से मिल सका । ओडिशा के तीन जिलों के गांवों में पानी की सप्लाई हो सके, इसके लिए हम ईपीसी कांट्रेक्ट के तहत एक प्रतिष्ठित कंपनी के साथ संयुक्त काम कर रहे हैं। साथ ही पांच साल तक उसके संचालन और रख-रखाव का भी कांट्रेक्ट है। ताजा ऑर्डर के मुताबिक कंपनी को ओड़िशा के ५५० से ज्यादा गांवों में पेयजल की आपूर्ति करनी है ।

हमारे एक संयुक्त काम इंफ्रास्ट्रक्चर प्रोजेक्ट में ग्रीनटेक मेगा फूड पार्क भी है। इसे हमने आंशिक स्वामित्व में रूपनगढ़, अजमेर (राजस्थान) में २०१४ में शुरू किया था । यह राजस्थान का पहला मेगा फूड पार्क है । इसकी स्थापना भारत सरकार के खाद्य प्रसंस्करण उद्योग मंत्रालय की मेगा फूड पार्क योजना के तहत की गई थी। पार्क करीब ९० एकड़ जमीन में डॉ. मुरलीधर खेतान फैला

है। इससे हजारों किसानों को प्राथमिक और केंद्रीय प्रसंस्करण और भंडारण की सुविधा उपलब्ध हो रही है। इससे पहले उचित सार-संभाल और भंडारण के अभाव में खाद्यान्न खराब हो जाता था । कोल्ड स्टोरेज और वेयरहाउस की सुविधा से अब खाद्यान्न को बचाना आसान हुआ है ।

कुंडली, हरियाणा में कंपनी का अपना वेयरहाउस (मालगोदाम) है। यह अस्सी हजार वर्ग फुट से ज्यादा जगह में बना हुआ है। यहां जल्दी खराब होने वाली खाद्य वस्तुएं, दवाइयां, पौष्टिक औषधियों को सुरक्षित रखने की पूरी सविधाएं हैं। क्रेंस, लिफ्ट्स, कोल्ड रूम्स आदि की सुविधाएं भी दे रखी हैं । हम यह जगह लीज पर देते हैं ।

कंपनी के प्रबंधकों में, मैं मुरलीधर खेतान कंपनी का अध्यक्ष और पूर्णकालिक निदेशक हूं । जयप्रकाश खेतान प्रबंध निदेशक है, बसंत कुमार खेतान और प्रदीप कुमार खेतान संयुक्त प्रबंध निदेशक हैं । जुगल किशोर अग्रवाल, शरद अग्रवाल, श्यामकनु महंत और उषा अग्रवाल गैर- कार्यकारी और स्वतंत्र निदेशक हैं ।

काजीरंगा विश्वविद्यालय

हमने असम सरकार से २३ मार्च २००९ को बीआईपीपीएल (ब्रह्मपुत्र इंफ्रा पावर प्राइवेट लिमिटेड) के नाम से बोर - डीकोराई की मुख्य नदी पर ४.७ एमडबल्यू बिजली बनाने का काम लिया था । काम करीब-करीब पूरा हो गया था। इस बीच जंगलात विभाग ने उसके विरोध में २५ मई २०१३ को सरकार को एक चिट्ठी लिख दी । असम सरकार के साथ वन विभाग का कोई झमेला था। इसके चलते २५ जून को सरकार ने प्रोजेक्ट बंद करवा दिया। बिजली बनाने का हमारा सपना टूट गया। उसके बाद हमने दूसरी लाइन में काम करने का मन बनाया। सभी की सहमति से शिक्षा क्षेत्र में जाने का निर्णय लिया । २० अप्रेल २००९ को 'द असम कांजीरंगा यूनिवर्सिटी' के नाम से शिक्षण संस्था रजिस्टर कराई । ११ अप्रेल २०१२ को असेंबली में असम प्राइवेट यूनिवर्सिटीज एक्ट २००७ के अधीन 'द असम कांजीरंगा यूनिवर्सिटी एक्ट २०१२' के नाम से अधिसूचना जारी हुई। इसी बीच हमने विश्वविद्यालय भवन का निर्माण कर दिया । जोरहाट शहर से बाहर एनएच ३७ के पास कोरईखोवा में हमने जमीन ली थी । भवन जून के पहले सप्ताह तक बन कर तैयार हो गया था । १४ जून २०१२ को असम के मुख्यमंत्री तरुणजी गोगोई ने इसका उद्घाटन किया। यहां इंजीनियरिंग और तकनीक, मैनेजमेंट, कंप्यूटिंग साइंस, बेसिक साइंस, सोशल साइंस और स्वास्थ्य विज्ञान की शिक्षा

डॉ. मुरलीधर खेतान

दी जाती है । संस्थापक होने के साथ-साथ मैं कुलाधिपति की हैसियत से भी इसका काम देख रहा हूं । हमने हमेशा पढ़ाई की गुणवत्ता पर जोर दिया है। हर साल करीब ५०० से ७०० विद्यार्थी प्रवेश लेते हैं। दो साल से कोविड-१९ की वजह से बच्चों के प्रवेश और पढ़ाई में बाधा पड़ी है। उम्मीद करता हूं, इस सन् २०१२ जोरहाट साल सब ठीक हो जाएगा। विश्वविद्यालय का

सारा काम मेरा दुसरा पुत्र तथा मेरी पौत्री रैनीदेखते हैं ।

एकल अभियान

Dr. M.D. Khetan In "Ekal Samannay Barg" Meeting of Friends of Tribals Society, Jorhat

स्वामी विवेकानंद का स्वप्न था कि जो बच्चे स्कूल नहीं जा सकते हैं, उनके लिए स्कूल को उनके घर तक जाना चाहिए। यानि पढ़ाई की व्यवस्था घर पर हो जाए। वे चाहते थे, भारत का बच्चा- बच्चा शिक्षित हो, चाहे वह ग्रामीण क्षेत्र का हो अथवा आदिवासी क्षेत्र का । विवेकानंद के इसी स्वप्न को रांची के भौतिक परमाणु विज्ञानी, प्रोफेसर राकेश पोपली ने अपना आदर्श वाक्य बनाया। उन्होंने १९८६ में गैर

Dr. M.D.Khetan In "Ekal Samannay Barg" Meeting of Friends of Tribals Society, Jorhat

डॉ. मुरलीधर खेतान

लाभकारी संगठन ईवीएफ (एकल विद्यालय फाउंडेशन ऑफ इंडिया) की स्थापना की । १९८९ में झारखंड के धनबाद में पोपली ने पहला एकल विद्यालय खोला। इसके साथ ही यहां के टुंडी ब्लॉक में गिरिडीह क्षेत्र के ३० पिछड़े गांवों में एकल विद्यालय खोले गए । एकल विद्यालय एक शिक्षक वाले विद्यालय हैं । इस काम में उनकी पत्नी बाल शिक्षा विशेषज्ञ रमा पोपली ने भी सहयोग किया था । शिक्षा से वंचित बच्चों की स्थिति समझने के लिए उन्होंने भारत ही नहीं, अमरीका के भी ग्रामीण और आदिवासी क्षेत्रों का जायजा लिया। दुर्भाग्य से जिस गति से यह काम शुरू हुआ था, राकेश पोपली के रक्त कैंसर से निधन हो जाने के बाद थोड़ा धीमा पड़ गया। उनका फाउंडेशन कई देशों में एकल विद्यालयों का संचालन कर रहा है । इसी अभियान के तहत जोरहाट अंचल में २७० एकल विद्यालय चल रहे हैं ।

लगभग १२ साल पहले वनबंधु परिषद के पूर्व अध्यक्ष रामेश्वरलाल जी काबरा (मुंबई) की उपस्थिति में मेरे जोरहाट वाले घर पर एक बैठक हुई थी। उसमें एकल अभियान के अगुआ अरुणजी बजाज भी मौजूद थे। एकल अभियान के लिए मैंने २०१६ जोरहाट अंचल के संस्थापक अध्यक्ष की जिम्मेदारी संभाली। तब से ही यह अभियान चल रहा

Dr. M.D. Khetan Honored Shri Shri Janardan Dev Goswai of North Kamalabari Satra on The Occasion

है। मैंने विश्व के सबसे बड़े नदी द्वीप माजुली में एकल अभियान शुरू किया। यहां भी २७० एकल विद्यालय हैं। एकल अभियान के मुहिम में मुझे बाबूलाल गगड़ और जुगल किशोर सिंघी का उल्लेखनीय सहयोग मिला। आज देशभर के २२ राज्यों के ६८६ जिलों के एक लाख दो हजार चार सौ नब्बे गांवों में एकल विद्यालय चल रहे हैं। हम बच्चों की शिक्षा के साथ ग्रामवासियों को आत्मनिर्भर बनाने की भी कोशिश कर रहे हैं ।

चाय बागान

हमने गोलाघाट के पास २०१७ में एक टी गार्डन लिया। रंगाजान और थोराजान बागान दोनों कुल ३२०० हैक्टेयर में हैं। कोरोना के कारण सही संभाल नहीं हो सकी । चाय के पत्ते खराब हो गये । बागान में खाली जमीन पर चाय के नए पौधे लगा रहे हैं। वे तीसरे साल पत्ते देना शुरू कर देंगे । रोजमर्रा के काम मेरा दूसरा पुत्र बसन्त देखता है ।

डॉ. मुरलीधर खेतान

गांव में पानी की सुविधा

गांवों में तालाब, कुएं, बावड़ियां ही जल के मुख्य स्रोत हुआ करते थे । बरसात से ही इनमें पानी की आवक होती थी । यही पानी पीने, नहाने-धोने के काम आता था। हमारे गांव बानूड़ा में भी ये ही पानी के साधन थे। पानी की बात चली है, तो मुझे वह हादसा याद आ रहा है, जब मेरे एक मित्र ने मेरी जान बचाई । १९५३ में असम से जब मैं पहली बार गांव आया, आषाढ़ का महीना था । उस साल बहुत ज्यादा बरसात हुई थी। ऐसी बारिश सालों से नहीं हुई थी। अच्छी बारिश से गांव के सारे तालाब लबालब भर गए थे। एक तालाब दक्षिण दिशा में है, वो सबसे बड़ा है। भरने पर बारहों महीने पानी रहता है । उसे सब लाम्बी तलाई कहते हैं । लाम्बी तलाई के नीचे उस वक्त रियासत की दी हुई ५००-६०० बीघा जमीन थी तथा उसी के बहाव से यह तलाई भरती थी। तालाब के चारों तरफ पत्थर और गारे की दीवार बनी हुई है । पानी आने के लिए दक्षिण की तरफ ५५ इंच का मोखा (नाला) या छेद बनाया हुआ है। उसी से सारा पानी उसमें आता है । छेद के पास पत्थरों से १५१५ फीट की एक जगह बनाई हुई है । लोग यहां बैठ कर नहाते हैं । जिन्हें तैरना आता है, वे तालाब के भीतर जाकर भी नहाते हैं। उत्तर दिशा में १० फीट चौड़ा और १५ फीट लंबा एक खुर्रा (उंची जगह) बनाया हुआ है । उससे आदमी या जानवर पानी के लिए जा सकते हैं । खुर्रा तलाई की जमीन पर जाकर उतरता है । उसी हिसाब से बनाया हुआ है। अब मैं असली बात पर आता हूं। बरसात ज्यादा होने से तालाब की पश्चिम दिशा की दीवार ३-४ फुट टूट गई थी । उससे तालाब का बहुत सारा पानी तालाब की उत्तर दिशा से बाहर निकल कर बहने लग गया था । इससे १५ - २० फुट गहरा और १० फीट चौड़ा गड्ढा हो गया था। पानी इतनी तेजी से बह रहा था कि किसी

को भी गड्ढे का अनुमान नहीं था। बरसात रुकने के बाद गांव के २०-२५ लोग देखने गए। मैं भी साथ गया । हम लोग नाले की दीवार के एक-डेढ़ फुट दूर से ही देख रहे थे। इतने में मेरे पास की करीब एक फुट जमीन टूट कर नाले में गिर गई, साथ ही मैं भी गिर गया। मुझे तैरना नहीं आता था । हमारे साथ मगनी रामजी शर्मा थे। वे तेजी से बहते नाले में तुरंत कूद पड़े और १०-१५ मिनट में मुझे बाहर निकाल लाए। हमारे साथ संयोग से एक वैद्यजी भी थे । उन्होंने मुझे उलटा-पुलटा किया। मेरे नाक- मुंह से पानी निकाला। एक-डेढ़ घंटे में मुझे होश आ गया। तब जाकर हम सब गांव लौटे। मगनी रामजी ने मुझे तो बचा लिया, पर उनका चश्मा उसी नाले में बह गया । २-३ दिन बाद धूप निकलने पर नाला सूख गया। दरअसल उसका पानी ४-५ मील बहकर एक दूसरे नाले में मिल गया था । पानी सूखने के बाद मैं मगनी रामजी के साथ तालाब के किनारे घूमने निकल गया। हम यह देखकर हैरान थे कि बेर की झाड़ी गें चश्मा अटका हुअ. है। पानी के उस तेज बहाव में चश्मे के मिलने की कोई उम्मीद नहीं थी। पर ईश्वर की मेहर हो तो कुछ भी संभव हो सकता है । मगनी रामजी अब इस दुनिया में नहीं हैं, पर उनकी यादें आज भी ताजा हैं। अपनी जान जोखिम में डालकर जिस तरह उन्होंने मुझे बचाया, उसे मेरा परिवार कभी नहीं भूल सकता ।

हमारे गांव में दूसरा तालाब पूर्व की ओर था। वह छोटा था, पर उसके नीचे दो सौ - ढाई सौ बीघा जमीन थी। तालाब के चारों ओर खेत थे । उसका पानी लगभग छह महीने काम आता था। तीसरा तालाब गांव से आधा मील दूर उत्तर दिशा में था । वह बहुत छोटा था । वह हमारे राजा की रियासत में नहीं था। सीकर रियासत में आता था। पर सीकर के गांव उससे दो-ढाई मील दूर थे, इसलिए उसका पानी हमारे गांव के ही काम आता था । तीन - चार महीना निकल जाता था। उसके नीचे ढाई सौ - तीन सौ बीघा जमीन थी । वहां सीकर रियासत के गांव वाले अपने मवेशी चराने लाते थे । हमारे गांव के मवेशी हमारे गांव के तालाबों की जमीन में चरने जाते हैं । अब कुछ वर्षों पहले सरकार ने तालाब की जमीन में एक प्राइमरी स्कूल खोल दी है। गांव के बच्चे वहां पढ़ते आते हैं ।

बारिश के दिनों में कुछ लोग छतों को साफ करके घड़े और छोटी टंकियां रख देते थे । वह पानी पीने के काम आता था । नहाने-धोने के लिए तो तालाब से लाना पड़ता था । बीकानेर. जोधपुर, जैसलमेर के लोग घर के नीचे बड़ी टंकी बनवाते हैं । उसी में बरसात का पानी भरकर पीने - नहाने के काम में लेते हैं ।

लाम्बी तलाई के पास ही श्मशान घाट है। वहीं गांव के लोगों का अंतिम संस्कार किया जाता है। अब तो उत्तरी पाल पर बालाजी का एक मंदिर बना दिया गया है । रात-दिन जागरण और प्रसादी वगैरह होते रहते हैं ।

बुजुर्गों ने कहा है कि जिस किसी के भी पास शक्ति और सामर्थ्य है, उन्हें औरों की मदद करनी चाहिए । इसी में जीवन की सार्थकता है । तालाब, कुएं, बावड़ियों का पानी घड़ों में भरकर लाना आसान नहीं था । बहुत मेहनत लगती थी । समय भी काफी लगता था । मैं अपने गांव की यह समस्या हल करना चाहता था। अपनी आमदनी से अपने गांव के लिए कुछ करना चाहता था। १९६५ में भारत-पाक युद्ध के समय मैं परिवार सहित कार से आया था और ३-४ महीने रहा । १९६२ में मेरा परिवार जोरहाट आ गया था । मेरा बेटा जयप्रकाश छठी कक्षा में था। बेटी सरोज डेढ़ साल की थी। दोनों का जन्म राजस्थान में हुआ था। स्कूल की गर्मियों की

छुट्टियां थीं। राजस्थान में भयंकर गर्मी पड़ती है। बरसात नहीं होती थी तो तालाब भी सूख जाते थे । गांव में एक कुआं था । ३-४ आदमी वहीं रहकर करीब २/३ घड़े पानी रोज लाते थे। बरसात में कुछ पानी तालाब से ले आते थे। वो भी काम आ जाता था । हमने गांव में पानी की व्यवस्था करने का विचार करके उसी साल काम शुरू कर दिया। सीकर में बद्रीनारायणजी सोडानी के यहां एक पम्प मिल गया था । पम्प पाइप के अलावा मोटर और अन्य खुदरा

सामान जो भी लगा सीकर से ले आए। साथ में मिस्त्री भी । ४-५ महीने में काम पूरा हो गया । कुएं के पास ही एक कोठी (टंकी) बनी हुई थी। मोटर की मदद से कुएं से पानी निकाल कर दिन में दो बार उस कोठी को भर देते थे।

टंकी के चारों तरफ नल लगवा दिए थे । हर समाज के लिए अलग अलग नल। नल के ऊपर दीवार पर नाम भी लिख दिए थे ताकि झगड़ा नहीं हो । उस समय सारा काम कराने के डेढ़- दो लाख रुपए लग गए। गांव से एक पैसा नहीं लिया । कुएं से कोठी में पानी भरने वाला आदमी, मिस्त्री का वेतन, और मोटर में लगने वाला डीजल आदि का पैसा भी हम लगा रहे थे । १९७१ तक कुएं से ही पानी ले जाना पड़ता था। १९७१ में टाटा कम्पनी के पाइप खरीद कर सारे गांव में लगवा दिए। उन्हें घर के नलों से जोड़ दिया। इस तरह पानी की व्यवस्था घरों में हो गई। जहां पाइप नहीं पहुंचे, नल घरों के सामने चौक में लगवा दिए । वहां से भी पानी भरना आसान हो गया। उस समय पाइप लगवाने का खर्चा करीब ४-५ लाख रुपया आया। वे पाइप आज भी दुरुस्त हैं । १९९१ से १९९५ तक सारा काम हमने चलाया, गांव से एक पैसा नहीं लिया । इसके बाद सारा काम सरकार ने संभाल लिया। गांव में बहुत बड़ी और ऊंची टंकी बनी हुई है। अब इससे सारे गांव में पानी पहुंचता है ।

समाज सेवा

अब कारोबार की चिंता नहीं थी । अच्छा चलने लगा था। यहां तक पहुंचने में घर-परिवार, मित्र - समाज सबका सहयोग रहा। समाज से जो लिया, उसे लौटाने का वक्त आ गया था । मारवाड़ी समाज हर क्षेत्र में पिछड़ा हुआ था। उसे आगे लाना था। जोरहाट की मारवाड़ी ठाकुरबाड़ी का १९७८ में चुनाव हुआ था। यूनाइटेड हार्डवेयर के पार्टनर रहे छगनलालाजी सिंघी के कहने पर मैंने पर्चा भरा। उस समय मैं यूनाइटेड हार्डवेयर से अलग हुआ ही था। मैं अपने हाईटेंशन इलेक्ट्रिकल्स वाले काम से चुनाव नहीं लड़ सकता था । मेरी फर्म रजिस्टर नहीं होने से उसकी यहां सदस्यता नहीं थी ।

<hr>

छगनलालजी ने मुझसे कहा, व्यापार में हम दोनों के अलग होने की बात केवल हमारे बीच में है ।

इसलिए आप यूनाइटे ड हार्डवेयर के नाम से पर्चा भर दें । मैंने भर दिया और सबसे ज्यादा मतों से जीता। मुझे इसका सभापति बनाया गया। मैं १९७८ से लेकर १९९२ तक, समाज की सर्वोच्च संस्था का १४ साल लगातार सभापति रहा। उसमें कई अहम फैसले सर्वसम्मति से लिए गए। समाज हित के कई काम करने का अवसर मिला। इसमें एक अहम फैसला मारवाड़ी ठाकुरबाड़ी की दाहिनी ओर की दुकानों में शौचालय बनाने का था । यह काम पिछले ४० साल से अटका हुआ था। लोग परेशान हो रहे थे । २० सितंबर १९९२ को नई समिति बना कर, उसकी जिम्मेदारी मुझे दे दी गई । और शौचालय का काम संपन्न हुआ ।

सन् २०११ में ठाकुरबाड़ी का सभापति जुगल किशोर सिंघी और सचिव माखनलाल गट्टाणी थे । ठाकुरबाड़ी की वार्षिक आम सभा में मैंने इसके भवन में एक लिफ्ट लगाने का प्रस्ताव रखा। इसे सहर्ष स्वीकार कर लिया गया। मैंने लिफ्ट लगवा दी। उसका उद्घाटन भी मुझ से ही ५ अक्टूबर २०१५ को कराया गया। दूसरी लिफ्ट प्रदीप कुमार सिंघल ने शताब्दी भवन के लिए दी । यह २०१४-१५ में बनी । उसका उद्घाटन भी मुझसे २५ फरवरी २०१९ को करवाया गया। मैंने अपनी तरफ से ज्यादा से ज्यादा आर्थिक सहयोग करने की कोशिश की ।

मैं अखिल भारतवर्षीय मारवाड़ी सम्मेलन का १९८७ से आजीवन सदस्य हूं । आजीवन मताधिकार का भी हक है। मैं इसके प्रमुख पत्र 'समाज विकास' का आजीवन सदस्य हूं। १५ जनवरी २००६ से १५ नवंबर २०१० तक मारवाड़ी सम्मेलन जोरहाट शाखा का ५ साल सभापति रहा । मेरे सभापतित्व में जोरहाट तथा आसपास के मारवाड़ी समाज की पहली टेलीफोन डायरेक्टरी निकाली गई । वह आज भी काम आ रही है । १५ नवंबर २०१० के बाद २६ अगस्त २०१८ तक मारवाड़ी सम्मेलन का सलाहकार रहा। २६ अगस्त २०१८ को मुझे इसका संरक्षक सदस्य नियुक्त किया गया। मैं महाराज अग्रसेनजी चेरिटेबल ट्रस्ट

गुवाहाटी का आजीवन सदस्य हूं। मारवाड़ी रिलीफ सोसाइटी जोरहाट शाखा का भी आजीवन सदस्य हूं ।

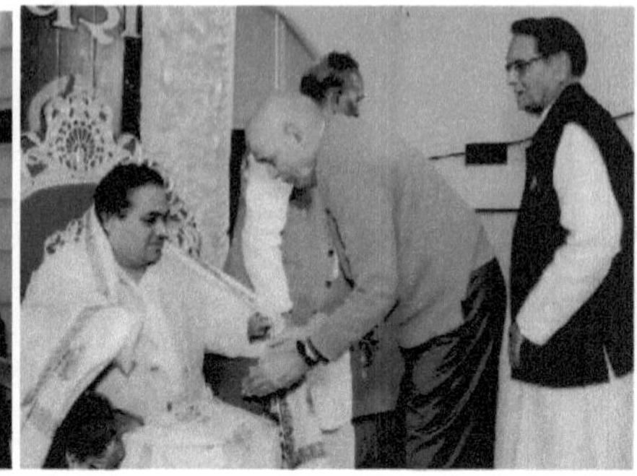

मैं जोरहाट में सन् १९७४-७५, १९७५-७६ और १९८१-८२ में अपर असम चैंबर ऑफ कॉमर्स की समिति का सदस्य रहा। इस हैसियत से हमने निर्णय लिया कि फेडरेशन ऑफ इंडिया चैंबर ऑफ कॉमर्स एंड इंडस्ट्री (फिक्की) के दिल्ली में होने वाले ४९वें अधिवेशन में जोरहाट से एक प्रतिनिधि मंडल भेजा जाय । सदस्यों की एक समिति बनाई गई । इसमें मेरे अलावा जुगल किशोर सिंघी, गोकुलचन्द जाजू, रामवतार बजाज, और रामेश्वरलाल जालान थे । अधिवेशन ३० अप्रेल ७६ से २ मई ७६ तक तीन दिन चला। (देखें तस्वीर)

मारवाड़ी ठाकुरबाड़ी में चैंबर भवन सन् १९४४ से था । १९७४-७५ में नई जगह लेकर खुद का चैंबर भवन बनाया गया। इसका उद्घाटन ११ अप्रेल १९७५ को असम के तत्कालीन राज्यपाल ललन प्रसाद सिंह ने किया था। फीता काटने की कैंची और प्लेट की नीलामी की गई थी। उन्हें मैंने ली । २०१४ से जोरहाट अग्रवाल सभा का सभापति रहा । आजीवन सदस्य भी हूं। अग्रवाल चेरिटेबल ट्रस्ट का १९८४ से ट्रस्टी हूं। ३० अगस्त २०१५ को मारवाड़ी चेरिटेबल ट्रस्ट का मैनेजिंग ट्रस्टी बनाया गया। समिति में विनोद सर्राफ डिप्टी मैनेजिंग ट्रस्टी हैं । खेमराज मोदी कैशियर । राधेश्यामजी सर्राफ, गोपाल पोद्दार, जुगलकिशोर सिंघी, महेश बेरिया, एम. पी. अग्रवाल (नामित) और भगवती प्रसाद गोयल सदस्य थे (१४ जनवरी २०१९ में भगवती प्रसाद गोयल का निधन हो जाने से उनकी जगह राजेश गोयल को सदस्य बनाया गया) । अग्रवाल सभा

का नया भवन बन रहा है । इसकी जिम्मेदारी विनोद सर्राफ (चेयरमैन), खेमराज मोदी (कैशियर), देबीदत्तजी बेरिया (सचिव), आनन्द अग्रवाल और रमेश सिंघी को दी गई है। पांच मंजिल के इस भवन में लिफ्ट लगाई जाएगी। काम चालू है ।

शिक्षण के क्षेत्र में मैं राष्ट्रभाषा विद्यालय से भी जुड़ा हुआ हूं । विद्यालय की स्वर्ण जयंती के अवसर पर एक नए भवन का निर्माण किया गया था । उसका नाम जुबुली भवन रखा गया। भवन निर्माण में कई लोगों ने आर्थिक सहयोग किया था। मैं भी उनमें शामिल था। गांव में हाई स्कूल का भवन बना तब भी सहयोग किया। गांव से जब बंशीधरजी भाईसाहब, पन्नालालजी तेजावत, लक्ष्मीनारायणजी माहेश्वरी और

Flag Hosting in Occasion of Maharaja Agarsen Jayanti, 2016

रुड़मलजी जैन जोरहाट आए, तो उन्हें स्कूल के लिए चंदा दिया। वापस जाते समय ये कलकत्ता होकर गये थे । कलकत्ता में सरदार शहर के सोहनलालजी दुगड़ रहते थे । उन्होंने भी स्कूल के वास्ते ५१०० रुपए दिए। स्कूल चलने लगा । खूब बच्चे पढ़ने आते । यह बात १९६५-६६ के आसपास की है। १९८० में हमने अपने गांव बानूड़ा में घर के सामने जानकीबल्लभजी का नया मन्दिर भी

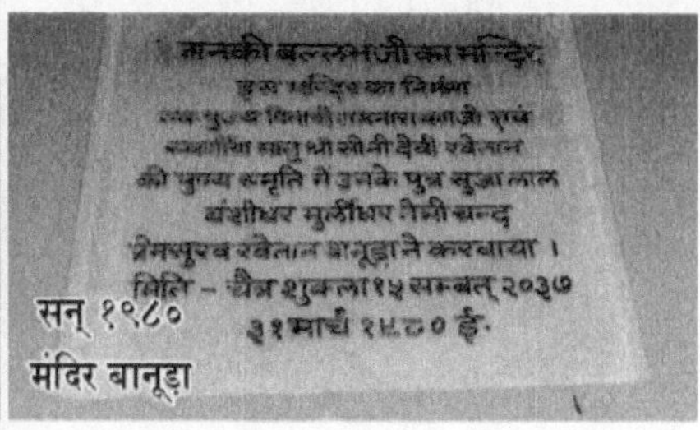

बनवाया । उस समय दो-ढाई लाख रुपए लग गए थे। मन्दिर में नल भी लगवा दिया था। गांव में गऊशाला के लिए भी सहयोग किया ।

आप सोच रहे होंगे कि मैं इतने सारे पद क्यों गिना रहा हूं । मैं अपने ये सभी पद और सदस्यता आपसे इसलिए साझा कर रहा हूं क्योंकि इनके जरिए मैं समाज के काम आ सका। लोगों के लिए कुछ कर सका। जैसा कि मैंने पहले भी कहा, मैं नहीं चाहता था कि हमारा मारवाड़ी समाज किसी भी क्षेत्र में पिछड़े। मैं उसका विकास चाहता था। प्रभु ने मुझे समर्थ भी बनाया था।

समाज-हित के कामों के लिए मुझे १६ सितंबर २०१६ को मंडी गोबिंदगढ़ (जिला फतेहगढ़ साहिब, पंजाब) स्थित देश भगत यूनिवर्सिटी के परिसर में डॉक्ट्रेट की मानद उपाधि से सम्मानित किया गया था । इसके लिए ३१ अक्टूबर २०१६ को दिपावली के मौके पर मारवाड़ी साफा पहनाकर बाबूलालजी गगड़ व तनसुखजी पंडित ने मेरा अभिनन्दन किया । (देखें तस्वीर) मुझे १० दिसंबर २०१७ को जीवनराम मूंगीदेवी गोयल के चेरिटेबल ट्रस्ट शिलाँग की ओर से लाइफटाइम अचीवमेंट अवार्ड भी दिया गया। इसमें असम के राज्यपाल जगदीश मुखी मुख्य अतिथि थे । वर्ष २००९ में जोरहाट में युवाओं की सबसे पुरानी और अग्रणी संस्था ने मुझे 'समाज का गौरव' की उपाधि से सम्मानित किया ।

सिंघी परिवार से आत्मीयता

बचपन से ही संयुक्त परिवार में रहे हैं । सबको साथ लेकर चलना सीखा है । चाहे अपने भाई-बहनों के साथ रहा या अपने खुद के परिवार के साथ। मैंने कभी भी निर्णय अकेले नहीं लिए। हर फैसले में परिवार की भागीदारी रही । मिल-बैठकर ही हमने फैसले लिए। परिवार का विस्तार जब मित्रों- परिचितों के बीच होने लगता है, या यूं कहिए कि मित्र और परिचित जब परिवार का अभिन्न

Dr. M.D. Khetan visits Christian Colony

हिस्सा बन जाते हैं, तो समझ लीजिए आत्मीयता चरम पर है। सफलताएं आपके

डॉ. मुरलीधर खेतान

कदम चूमना चाहती हैं। सिंघी परिवार से मेरी आत्मीयता कुछ ऐसी ही थी । १९५९ में यूनाइटेड हार्डवेयर में साझेदारी के समय मैं इनके संपर्क में आया था। आज भी आना- जाना सब पहले की तरह है। खासकर जुगल किशोर, ईश्वरलाल और रमेश सिंघी से मेरा ज्यादा लगाव है। जुगल किशोर से प्रेम १९५९ से ही है । तब वो पढ़ता था। मैं छगनलाल और मदनलाल सिंघी भाइयों के साथ साझेदारी में तो काम कर ही रहा था। दोनों वक्त भोजन भी उनके यहीं करता था क्योंकि अकेला था। खाने का कोई बन्दोबस्त नहीं था। तभी से उससे मेरी नजदीकियां हैं। फिक्की के ४९ वें अधिवेशन में हम साथ गए थे। मैं और जुगल नामरूप और दीमापुर तो कई बार साथ गये । कोहिमा, मणिपुर और इम्फाल भी साथ गए थे। नागालैंड, मणिपुर में हमारा बिजली का सामान सप्लाई करने का काम था । १३ दिसंबर १९७५ में जयप्रकाश के विवाह में भी वह साथ था। पहले आई. सी बोथरा (आईटी वकील) के घर हर रविवार ताश खेलते थे। तब भी जुगल आया करता था । १९७९ में हाईटेंशन इलेक्ट्रिकल्स की दुकान खोलने के बाद तो रोजाना शाम के समय ताश खेलते थे। आज भी खेलते हैं । ८ जुलाई १९६० को जुगल किशोर, बजरंगलाल और ईश्वरलाल तीनों मैट्रिक की परीक्षा देकर सीकर से बस में बानूड़ा गये थे। उस समय मैं और मेरा परिवार बानूड़ा ही था। दो दिन रहकर १० जुलाई १९६० को बानूड़ा से वापस सीकर आकर बम्बई चले गये । उसकी पत्नी तारामणि और बच्चे अक्सर जुगल के साथ गांव आते रहते थे । अपनी कार से उन्हें पहुंचाने का मैं खास खयाल रखता था ताकि वे परेशान नहीं हों। एक बार की बात है कि जुगल को सीकर से जोराहट सड़क द्वारा कार से भिजवाया था। जब जुगल किशोर जेबी कॉलेज में बीकॉम पढ़ रहा था, मेरा भाई प्रेमसुख भी उसके साथ था। इससे घनिष्ठता और बढ़ गई थी । होली - दीवाली घर पर आना-जाना, शादी-ब्याह आदि मौकों में शामिल होना । सलाह-मशविरे में साथ, तो दुख-सुख में भी साथ ।

सेहतमंद बर्तन भूल गए !

अब मैं एक बार उन दिनों में लौटना चाहता हूं जब मैं १०-१५ साल का था । पीतल की थाली में भोजन करते थे। छाछ तांबे के गिलास में पीते और पानी पीतल के गिलास में । कारण छाछ पीतल के गिलास में खराब हो जाती है। हर घर में तांबे और पीतल की बड़ी-बड़ी २- ४ कोठियां पानी के लिए रहती

थीं। तांबे का एक ही बड़ा गिलास रहता था। उस में ही पीने का पानी रखते थे । तांबे का नहीं तो पीतल का तो सबके ही घर में रहता था । गरीब से गरीब घर में। शादी-ब्याह के मौकों पर तांबे या पीतल की कोठी में पानी भर कर रख देते थे । उसे काठ के तख्ते से ढककर बाल्टी और लौटा रख देते ताकि जनेती (बराती) अपने आप पानी लेकर नहा लें । उस वक्त बरात में जाने के लिए एक धोती सेनगुप्ता की रखते । एक जोड़ी धोती का दाम एक रुपया बारह आना होता था। एक कमीज सिलवाकर रखते थे। बरात में एक ही धोती ले जाते थे। नहाने से पहले उसे धोकर दो आदमी मिलकर सुखा लेते। उतनी देर लाल रंग का गमछा लपेट कर रखते थे । धोती सूख जाने पर नहाते । फिर धोती और कमीज पहन, बन- ठन कर जीमने जाते। उस वक्त तांबे का भाव १ रुपया और पीतल का आठ आना सेर था। फिर धीरे-धीरे लोहे पर कलई की हुई कोठियां आने लगीं । कारण तांबा और पीतल का दाम बढ़ गया था । सन्

डॉ. मुरलीधर खेतान

१९३४-४० तक तो चांदी के रुपए ही चलते थे। धीरे-धीरे आधी चांदी और आधा जस्ते का रुपया, अठन्नी और चवन्नी बनने लगे । १९४७ में भारत आजाद होने के बाद तांबे के एक आना, दो आना, चार आना, आठ आना और रुपया में जस्ता बढ़ने लगा था। तांबे के ये पैसे अभी भी मेरे पास हैं। पहले तांबे का पैसा मोटा आता था। फिर पतला बनने लगा। बाद में मामूली तांबा देकर बीच में छेद रख कर आने लगे । धीरे-धीरे एक रुपया, दो रुपए, पांच रुपए, दस रुपए, सौ रुपए, हजार रुपए, पांच हजार रुपए और दस हजार रुपए के नोट आने लगे । १६ जनवरी १९७८ को तत्कालीन प्रधानमंत्री मोरारजी देसाई ने एक हजार, पांच हजार और दस हजार के नोटों को बंद करवा दिया था । काले धन पर अंकुश लगाने के लिए। जो बैंक में जमा करवा सके, उनके वे नोट काम में आ गए। बाकी के नोट रद्दी बन कर रह गए।

तांबा और पीतल का उपयोग सेहत के लिए अच्छा होता है । पर लोग स्टेनलेस स्टील काम में लेने लगे हैं । कहीं ऐसा नहीं हो कि ये इतिहास की बातें बन कर रह जाएं। पहले फूटी कौड़ी की भी कीमत थी। तीन फूटी कौड़ी में एक साबुत कौड़ी आ जाती थी। गांव में किसी के बच्चे का जन्म होता, तो उसके गले में फूटी कौड़ी डोरे में पिरोकर पहनाते थे। नजर लगने से बचाने के लिए। कहावत है, कौड़ी के मोल हाथी जाए। कोई लेने वाला नही मिलता था। कौड़ी के बाद रति होती थी, रति के बाद पाई, पाई के बाद पैसे। इसके बाद चार पैसे का एक आना और सोलह आने का एक रुपया होता था । ६४ पैसे का एक रुपया होता था, जो तांबे का मोटा पैसा होता था ।

शादियों का वो जमाना और हमारी शरारतें

बंशीधर भाई की बरात किशनगढ़ रेनवाल के पास करड़ गांव में भूरामलजी शिवदयाल गोयल के यहां गई थी। बरात में मैं भी गया था। मुझे आज भी थोड़ा-थोड़ा याद है । उस समय बरात तीन दिन रुकती थी । बीन (दूल्हा) राजा तथा बिनायक के लिए बैलगाड़ी का रथ बनाया जाता। वे उसमें जाते और बाकी जनेती (बराती) ऊंटों पर । करड़ पहुंचने के बाद रथ को एक तरफ खड़ा कर दिया। मैं और साथ का एक लड़का जीमने के बाद रथ में जाकर लेट गए और परदे गिरा दिए। रास्ते की थकान थी, भरपेट जीमे हुए थे, सो गहरी नींद आ गई। हम बच्चे ही तो थे, १२ बजे सोए जो दोपहर ढलने तक सोए रहे। जब काफी समय हो गया और हम नजर नहीं आए तो बरात में हल्ला मच गया कि हमारे दो टाबर नहीं मिल रहे हैं । गांव में घर-घर ढूंढ़ते फिरे । पर हम मिलते कहां से ! जहां सोए थे, वहां की तो कोई सोच भी नहीं सकता था । बराती - घराती सब चिंता करने लगे । तरह-तरह की आशंकाएं होने लगीं। कहीं दूसरे गांव के आदमी तो उठाकर नहीं ले गए। शाम ५-६ बजे के करीब

डॉ. मुरलीधर खेतान

जब पेट में चूहे दौड़ने लगे, प्यास भी सताने लगी तब हमारी आंख खुली। रथ से नीचे उतरे और घरवालों से पानी और कुछ खाने को मांगा। हम दोनों को अचानक प्रकट हुए देखकर वे हैरान थे और बेहद नाराज भी। पूछा, 'अति देर कठे हा, म्हाको तो होश उड़गो ।' हम बोले, 'म्हे तो अठे ही रथ में सुताहा ।' तब सबकी जान में जान आई। घरवालों ने डांटा और पिटाई भी हुई। बच्चे ही तो थे, खा-पीकर फिर से खेलने लग गए। २-४ बच्चे और आ गए थे ।

उन दिनों बरातियों के नाश्ते के लिए लड्डू, पेठा, सुंवाली (मठरी), और भुजिया बनता था। बराती जान (बरात) में जाते समय लाल रंग का एक गमछा साथ ले जाते थे। जब उन्हें सुबह चार लड्डू, थोड़े पेठे, ४ सुंवाली और एक धोबो भर भुजिया देते, तो वे उसे टाबरों के लिए गमछे में बांध लेते थे। नाश्ता ८ बजे देते और जीमण १ बजे होता । शाम का नाश्ता ५ बजे मिलता । उन्हें फिर टाबरों के लिए गमछे में बांध लेते। रात का खाना ८ बजे होता। घर में चौक बड़ा होने पर भी बरातियों को जीमने के लिए वहां नहीं बैठाते थे । चौक में दूल्हे राजा के लिए थाम रोपा जाता था । फेरे होने के बाद थाम के नीचे दूल्हा अपने २-४ साथियों के साथ खाना खाता और बाकी बराती छत पर जीमते। उनके लिए पांतियां (दरियां) बिछाई जातीं और पत्तल में खाना परोसते । जीमण में पत्तों से बनी पत्तलें और दोने ही काम में लेते थे । तब आज की तरह न तो कुर्सी टेबल थी, न थाली, और न ही प्लास्टिक और थर्मो कोल की पत्तलें ।

तीन दिन बरात रहती । मिठाई में केवल लड्डू ही बनते थे । बाकी एक दिन खीचड़ा करके जिमा देते। दूसरे दिन दाल-चूरमा होता, तो कभी सीरा (आटे का हलवा) और सुंसवा (सूखे मसालेदार काले चने) । आज की तरह न तो व्यंजनों की विविधता थी और न ही परोसने के तामझाम । कोई खास शादी होती तो जलेबी के दर्शन हो जाते । जलेबी को ऊंची मिठाई में आंका जाता था।

खेतों की मौज-मस्ती

जब मैं छोटा था, अपने खेत में खूब जाता था। वहीं दोपहर में किसी पेड़ के नीचे दोस्तों के साथ बैठ जाता। खास करके खेजड़ी का पेड़ होता था । अच्छी हवा चलती थी। सब मिलकर बाजरा और मक्के के सिट्टे सेंककर खाते । काकड़ी, मतीरा खाते । मोठ की फली का आनंद लेते। शाम के समय घर लौटते तब गायों के लिए घास बांध लेते और उसे माथे पर रख कर पैदल आते । हमारा खेत गांव से एक-डेढ़ मील दूर था । खेत के तालाब में नहाते । अब सब बातें इतिहास हो गई हैं। किसानों के खेत हैं । बनियों - ब्राह्मणों के नहीं रहे, बिक गए । कास्तकारों ने सारी जमीनें खरीद लीं। मैं २० साल का हुआ तब तक खेतों में जाना-आना लगा रहा। १९५० में जोरहाट जाने के बाद एक दो बर्ष से छुट्टी मिलती । १ - २ महीने के लिए राजस्थान जाता । तब कहीं जाकर खेतों की सूरत दिखती । बाजरा - मोठ की फली और सिट्टों का फिर से आनंद लेते । सन् १९८० तक तो गांव में आने-जाने का काम पड़ता रहा । फिर धीरे धीरे बंद हो गया। जोरहाट से गांव आते, ननिहाल या बहन- बेटी से मिलने २-४ कोस जाना होता, तो पैदल ही निकल पड़ते थे । उस वक्त न तो लूटपाट थी और न कोई बदमाशी होती । सो डर की कोई बात नहीं

डॉ. मुरलीधर खेतान

थी । एक दूसरे के लिए अपनापन था । मरण - परण सब मौकों पर गांव के लड़के हाजिर हो जाते । मिलकर काम करते थे । यहां तक कि बरतनों की सफाई भी कर लेते थे । उस जमाने में नौकर-चाकर न तो मिलते थे और न ही काम करने में किसी बच्चे को शर्म थी ।

जब शास्त्रीजी को देखा

१९६५ में भारत-पाक युद्ध के दौरान मैं जोरहाट से अपने गांव बानूड़ा कार से आया था। बनारस के पास कुछ बदमाशों ने हमारी गाड़ी पर पथराव करना शुरू कर दिया था। हम जैसे-तैसे वहां से बचकर लखनऊ पहुंचे। अपने जानकार दमाणीजी के घर रुके। पथराव से विंड स्क्रीन टूट गई थी। उसे ठीक करवा कर दूसरे दिन सवेरे पांच बजे निकल कर आगरा पहुंचे। वहां ताजमहल और अन्य दर्शनीय स्थल देखे। फिर अपने गांव पहुंचे और आराम किया। युद्ध के कारण हम सब एक महीना गांव रुके रहे। ऑल इंडिया रेडियो पर खबरें बराबर सुन रहे थे। तब एक ही रेडियो था, वह भी हमारी दुकान पर। सब खबरें सुनने के लिए वहीं इकट्ठा होते थे। उस वक्त तत्कालीन प्रधानमंत्री लाल बहादुर शास्त्री जयपुर आए थे। अलबर्ट हॉल पर उनका भाषण था। हम भी गए। उस समय देश में भयंकर सूखा पड़ा। देश को अनाज के लिए अमरीका या अन्य किसी देश के आगे हाथ न फैलाना पड़े, इसके लिए उन्होंने देशवासियों से सप्ताह में एक दिन व्रत रखने की अपील की। कृषि उत्पादन में आत्मनिर्भरता के लिए 'जय जवान जय किसान' का नारा भी दिया।

डॉ. मुरलीधर खेतान

विदेश यात्राएँ

मैं देश के बाहर कई बार गया । कभी व्यावसायिक उद्देश्य से, तो कभी परिवार के साथ। इन यात्राओं के दौरान जहां मौज-मस्ती की वहीं काफी कुछ सीखने को भी मिला। मेरी सबसे पहली विदेश यात्रा वर्ष १९८९ में दक्षिण कोरिया की थी। श्री आर. पी. गोयल के साथ २५ सितंबर से २ अक्टूबर तक हफ्तेभर की यात्रा

सन् १९८९, जापान

सन् १९८९, कोरिया

थी। गोयल साहब अब कायम नहीं हैं । सियोल में हमने वहां की नामचीन कंपनी सीसाँ देखी। यहां अत्याधुनिक तकनीक के ३६० वीआर कैमरे और लेजर स्कैनर बनते हैं। इसके बाद जापान और सिंगापुर की यात्रा भी व्यावसायिक मकसद से थी । जापान वर्ष १९९० में २३ अप्रैल को गया था और २५ अप्रैल को लौट आया। वहां एनजीके इंसुलेटर्स के चेयरमैन से मिला और फैक्ट्री भी गया । सिंगापुर १३ मार्च १९९२ को एक दिन के लिए गया था। वहां ऐलुमिनियम रॉड्स और वायर्स से संबंधित बातचीत करनी थी। जापान और सिंगापुर की यात्राओं में भी गोयल साहब मेरे साथ थे।

सन् १९८९, जापान

सन् १९८९, जापान

इसके बाद मैं ऑस्ट्रेलिया यात्रा पर अपने परिवार के साथ गया । हम लोग १४ अगस्त २००६ को वहां पहुंचे और २३ अगस्त को लौट आए थे । सिडनी, गोल्ड कॉस्ट कान्स, द ग्रेट बरियर रीफ, जाबुकई आदिवासी गांव देखने के बाद हॉट एयर गुब्बारों (सिडनी में) का लुत्फ भी लिया। इसके बाद मलेशिया, थाइलैंड और सिंगापुर गया। ये सभी यात्राएं मैंने परिवार के साथ २००७ और २०११ में की थीं।

हमारे कुल देवी-देवता

जीण माता हमारी कुल देवी हैं। इसका भी व्यावहारिक कारण रहा होगा। आज से डेढ़ सौ साल पहले सालासर बालाजी, रामदेव बाबा, खाटू श्यामजी जाने के कोई साधन नहीं थे। जीण माता का मंदिर गांव से डेढ़-दो मील दूर ही है। करीब होने के कारण जात वगैरह के संस्कार वहीं होने लगे। जीण माता को ही सब कुल देवी मानने लगे। बुजुर्गों की डाली परंपरा आज भी चल रही है। हालांकि आज हम सभी जगह माथा टेकने जाते हैं । झुंझनू की रानी सती माता के भी जाते हैं । सालासर हमारे गांव से ९० किलोमीटर है, रामदेवरा ४०० किलोमीटर, और खाटू श्यामजी ८५ सालासर

बालाजी किलोमीटर। हम सभी को मानते हैं, पर श्याम बाबा में हमारी कुछ ज्यादा ही आस्था है। असम के तिनसुकिया जिले के पानीतोला शहर में श्याम बाबा का एक मंदिर है । पानीतोला के श्याम बाबा में हमारे पूरे परिवार की बहुत आस्था है । मंदिर की पुजारिन को भी हम खूब मानते थे । उन्हें हम बुआजी कहते थे । उनकी कही बातें प्रायः सच होती थीं। वे अब नहीं रहीं ।

अब उनका बेटा पूजा करता है। हम सभी साल में तीन-चार बार मंदिर में इकट्ठा होते हैं। सवामणि के लिए । दर्शन के लिए करीब-करीब हर मंगलवार को जाते ही हैं। इस दिन भक्तों का तांता लगा रहता है । मुझे इस समय मेरे जीवन की सबसे सुखद घड़ी याद आ रही है, जब मेरे घर में २५ साल बाद लड़के ने जन्म लिया था । १९९४ में मेरा छोटा बेटा प्रदीप अपनी पढ़ाई करके सीकर आ गया था । मार्च १९९५ में उसे बेटा हुआ था। प्रदीप के जन्म के बाद घर में पहली बार लड़का (मेरा पौत्र) हुआ था । उसके जात-जड़ुला

संस्कार के लिए हम सब जोरहाट से सीकर आए । १९९० में बने अपने घर पर रुके । मेरी पत्नी, जय प्रकाश, रंजना, बसंत, स्नेहा, उनके बच्चे..हम सब हवाई जहाज से पहले दिल्ली आए। यहां एक बस बुक करवा रखी थी । उससे सीकर गए। बस हमारे साथ १०-१२ दिन रही। जीण माता, सालासर, खाटू श्याम आदि कई जगह गए। पूजा-अर्चना की । सालासर मंदिर से अपनी इच्छा से दो किलोमीटर पैदल चला। उस समय मैं ६४ का था। २५ साल बाद घर में किसी लड़के का जन्म हुआ था । मेरे पौत्र का । उसकी खुशी और उत्साह था । फिर वहां से रामदेवरा गए। रामदेव बाबा का मेला भरा हुआ था। काफी भीड़ थी । हमने रात पोखरण की एक जैन धर्मशाला में बिताई । पुरुष कुएं के पास चबूतरे पर सोए और महिलाएं एक कमरे में। सुबह चाय-नाश्ता करके रामदेवरा गए। बाबा के दर्शन किए। और रात में सीकर लौट आए। दो-तीन दिन रुक कर हम दिल्ली पहुंचे और हवाई जहाज से ही जोरहाट आ गए।

अलाव पर दुख-सुख की बातें

हमारी गांव वाली दुकान के पास सर्दियों में रात के समय कऊं (अलाव) जलाते थे । जमादारनी जलने लायक ओगदा (घास-फूस, सूखे पत्तों, टहनियों का कचरा) जमा करके अलाव की जगह पर रख जाती थी। शाम को नाई बाबा आता और साढ़े छह बजे तक कऊं जला देता था । यहां गांव के सभी बूढ़े, बच्चे, जवान इकट्ठे होते थे । वे सब अपनी दुख- सुख की बातें करते। गांव का हाल बताते । किस्से कहानियां रात के ११ बजे तक चलती रहती थीं । जब मैं १५ साल का था, गांव वाले दो बातें खास तौर पर किया करते थे। एक छपनिया अकाल की और दूसरी स्पेनिश फ्लू की । छपनिया अकाल सन् १८९९ में पड़ा था । उस समय विक्रम संवत् १९५६ था इसलिए लोकभाषा में यह छपनिया अकाल के नाम से कुख्यात है । यह राजस्थान का भीषणतम अकाल था, जिसे त्रिकाल भी कहते हैं । अन्न, पानी, चारा तीनों का अकाल पड़ गया था । उस वर्ष एक बूंद पानी नहीं बरसा । तालाब, कुएं, बावड़ी सब सूख गए थे। लोग पानी को तरस गए। खेतों में बिल्कुल पैदा नहीं हुई। लोग भूख-प्यास से मरने लगे। यही हाल मवेशियों का था। बुजुर्ग बताते कि पेट

भराई के लिए खेजड़ी, बवूल, पीपल, बड़ आदि की छाल ही खाने लगे थे। कभी कभार खाने का कुछ सामान राजा साहब भिजवा देते थे । इस अकाल से राजस्थान के अलावा पंजाब, गुजरात और मध्य भारत प्रभावित हुए। भूख से लाखों की संख्या में लोग मर गए । अन्न-जल के अभाव में उपजी बीमारियों ने भी जानें लीं। जो बचे, वे हड्डियों के ढांचे रह गए थे। जैसे-तैसे साल निकला। अगले साल बरसात आयी, तब कहीं जाकर दुर्भिक्ष अकाल से मुक्ति मिली। पेट भर खाने को मिला ।

दूसरी त्रासदी थी स्पेनिश फ्लू की महामारी । सन् १९१८ में इसने ऐसा कहर ढाया कि करोड़ों लोग मर गए । विश्व में ५ करोड़ तो भारत में एक करोड़ से ज्यादा लोगों की जानें गई (स्रोत - गूगल) । अंतिम संस्कार तक के लिए आदमी नहीं मिलते थे । फ्लू का संक्रमण इतना भयंकर था कि कई घर खाली हो गये। फ्लू से बचने के लिए लोग खेतों में चले गए। दो-चार महीने वहीं रहे । महामारी खत्म हुई तब वापस आए । मेरा तो उस समय जन्म भी नहीं हुआ था। जो सुना वही बता रहा हूं, पर है शत प्रतिशत सही ।

गांव में कऊं अपनापन और प्रेम के विस्तार का भी ठिकाना था । किसी परिवार में अनबन या लड़ाई हो जाती, कोई दो परिवार एक दूसरे के घर जाना-आना बंद कर देते, तो गांव का पंच उन परिवारों में सुलह करवा देता था।

कोरोना का दौर

ईश्वर ने हमें २०२० - २१ में वह त्रासदी भी दिखा दी, जो जीवन के नौ दशकों में नहीं देखी थी। सोच भी नहीं सकते थे कि कोविड - १९ की ऐसी महामारी आएगी, जो विश्वभर में हाहाकार मचा देगी । महामारी से विश्वभर में १९ नवम्बर २०२१ तक ५, १४८, १०० और भारत में ४,६५,०८२ लोग मर गए (स्रोत: वर्डोमीटर डॉट कॉम) । मौत का यह मंजर अब भी जारी है । विडंबना यह है कि महामारी का अब तक कोई पुख्ता इलाज नहीं है । चिकित्सकों के प्रयास अंधेरे में तीर मारने जैसे थे। बचाव के लिए सभी देशों ने अपने यहां लॉकडाउन लगाया ताकि लोग घरों में सुरक्षित रहें । उन्हें महामारी का संक्रमण नहीं हो । अपने भारत में भी लगाया गया । गाइडलाइंस भी जारी की गईं। हमने भी अपनी सभी फैक्ट्रियों में सवेतन अवकाश घोषित कर दिया था । काम-धंधे सब ठप हो गए थे। स्वास्थ्य मंत्री हिमंत विश्व शर्मा के अनुरोध पर हमने काजीरंगा विश्वविद्यालय को कोरोना मरीजों के इलाज के लिए खोल दिया था। इस बीच जो रिसर्च हुए, उनके आधार पर इलाज शुरू हुआ, टीके भी बनाए गए । पर वे भी शत प्रतिशत कारगर नहीं हैं । कोरोना की दूसरी लहर ने युवाओं को नहीं बख्शा। और अब तीसरी लहर बच्चों की जान की दुश्मन बन गई है। खबर तो यह भी है कि कोरोना का एक और वेरिएंट डेल्टा प्लस भारत में प्रवेश कर चुका है । इसे पहले वालों से ज्यादा खतरनाक बताया जा रहा है ।

मैं और मेरी पत्नी सोहनी देवी भी कोरोना की पहली लहर की गिरफ्त में आ गए थे। परिवार पर मुसीबतों का पहाड़ तो तब टूट पड़ा जब मेरी हमसफर, मेरी पत्नी सोहनी महामारी से जूझते हुए २४ अक्टूबर २०२० को सुबह १० बजकर २० मिनट पर चल बसी। मैं ठीक हो गया था। मैंने जीवन

में कई तकलीफें देखी हैं, पर कभी खुद को इतना लाचार महसूस नहीं किया था। वह मेरे दुख-सुख की संगी थी । उसके जाने ने मेरे जीवन को रिक्त कर दिया है । कभी नहीं भरने वाला खालीपन । पर जीवन रुकता नहीं है । सांसें हैं तब तक चलना है । काम करते रहना है । यही जीवन है ।

मेरा परिवार

❋ डॉ. मुरलीधर खेतान

जन्म: १०.११.१९३१

पत्नी: स्व. सोहनी देवी खेतान

जन्म: १५.८.१९३५

निधन: २४ अक्टूबर २०२०

पिता: स्व. महादेव जी अग्रवाल (मंढा सुरेरा वाले)

विवाह : ६. ६. १९५०

❋ जयप्रकाश खेतान (पुत्र)

जन्म: २५.४.१९५४

पत्नी: रंजना खेतान

जन्म: ३०.१.१९५७

पिता: चिरंजीलाल जी गाड़ोदिया (मोरान वाले)

विवाह: १३.१२.१९७५

❋ **सरोज साहेवाला (पुत्री)**

जन्म: २९.५.१९६२

पति: गजानन्द साहेवाला (वरिष्ठ वकील, गुवाहाटी हाईकोर्ट)

जन्म: २६.४.१९५४

पिता: स्व. सूरजमल जी साहेवाला (बोरसिला वाले)

विवाह: २३.११.१९८१

❋ **उर्मिला क्याल (पुत्री)**

जन्म: १३.५.१९६४

पति: डॉ. अशोक कुमार क्याल, न्यूरो फिजीशियन, एमडी, डीएम

जन्म: १.११.१९५४

पिता: स्व. बासुदेव जी क्याल (होजाई वाले)

विवाह: ८.२.१९८५

❋ **बसन्त कुमार खेतान**

जन्म: १५.१२.१९६७

पत्नी: स्नेहा खेतान

जन्म: १६.१०.१९६७

पिता: प्रहलाद राय जी बाजारी (माकूम वाले)

विवाह: १६.५.१९९१

❋ **प्रदीप खेतान**

जन्म: २८.६.१९६९

पत्नी: कविता खेतान

जन्म: १६.८.१९७२

पिता: रतन लाल जी बजाज (दिल्ली)

विवाह: १०.१२.१९९३

✳ **जयप्रकाश की संतानें**

✳ **रश्मि खेतान सर्राफ**

जन्म:१३.१०.१९७७ (जोरहाट)

पति: अमित सर्राफ

जन्म: ८.२.१९७३

विवाह: २.७.१९९८ (गुवाहाटी)

पुत्र: मनहन सर्राफ

जन्म: ८.६.२०००

✳ **पायल खेतान खदरिया**

जन्म: २१.८.१९७९ (जोरहाट)

पति: डॉ. अविनाश खदरिया (नोगांव)

जन्म: २२.४.१९७५

विवाह: २२.६.२००४

पुत्री: राजवी खदरिया

जन्म: २.५.२००७

✳ **निधि खेतान शाह**

जन्म: ८.७.१९८१(जोरहाट)

पति: नितिन शाह

जन्म: २७.३.१९८०

विवाह: १२.६.२००६

पुत्र: वेदांग शाह

जन्म: १६.३.२०१२

✳ **दीपज्योति खेतान मोतियानी**

जन्म: २२.१.१९८३ (जोरहाट)

पति: कुशल मोतियानी

जन्म: ७.६.१९८३

विवाह: ६.१२.२००७ (जयपुर)

पुत्री: सारा मोतियानी

जन्म: २.३.२०११

सरोज साहेवाला की संतानें

✳ **सिमी साहेवाला मोदी**

जन्म: १४.१०.१९८२

पति: अविनाश मोदी

जन्म: १०.३.१९७६

विवाह: २६.१.२००६

पुत्री: पहल मोदी जन्म: ९.७.२००८

पुत्री: रिया मोदी जन्म: ३०.१२.२०१०

✳ **श्वेता साहेवाला बावरी**

जन्म: १५.२.१९८६

पति: गौरव बावरी

जन्म: १०.२.१९८६

विवाह: २९.११.२००९

पुत्र: श्रेय बावरी जन्म: ९.११.२०१६

❋ मयंक साहेवाला

जन्म: २३.७.१९९३

पत्नी: तनुषा साहेवाला

जन्म: १६.१०.१९९२

विवाह: १७.४.२०१९

ऊर्मिला क्याल की संतानें

❋ नेहा क्याल

जन्म: ९.४.१९८६

पति: अंकित अग्रवाल

जन्म: ३१.८.१९८५

विवाह: २४.६.२०१२

पुत्र: हियांश अग्रवाल

जन्म: १४.४.२०१९

❋ अभिषेक क्याल

जन्म: २५.८.१९८८

पत्नी: गरिमा क्याल

जन्म: ९.२.१९८९

विवाह: १३.१२.२०१५

बसन्त कुमार खेतान की संतानें

❋ रेनी खेतान जन्म: २६.४.१९९२

❋ मेघना खेतान जन्म: ६.१.१९९९

प्रदीप खेतान की संतानें

✳ श्रेष्ठ खेतान

जन्म: ३१.३.१९९५

पत्नी: सृष्टि खेतान

पिता : अशोक जी मित्तल (जालन्धर वाले)

जन्म: १०.४.१९९६

विवाह: ३०.४.२०२१

✳ विशेष खेतान

जन्म: १५.१.१९९८

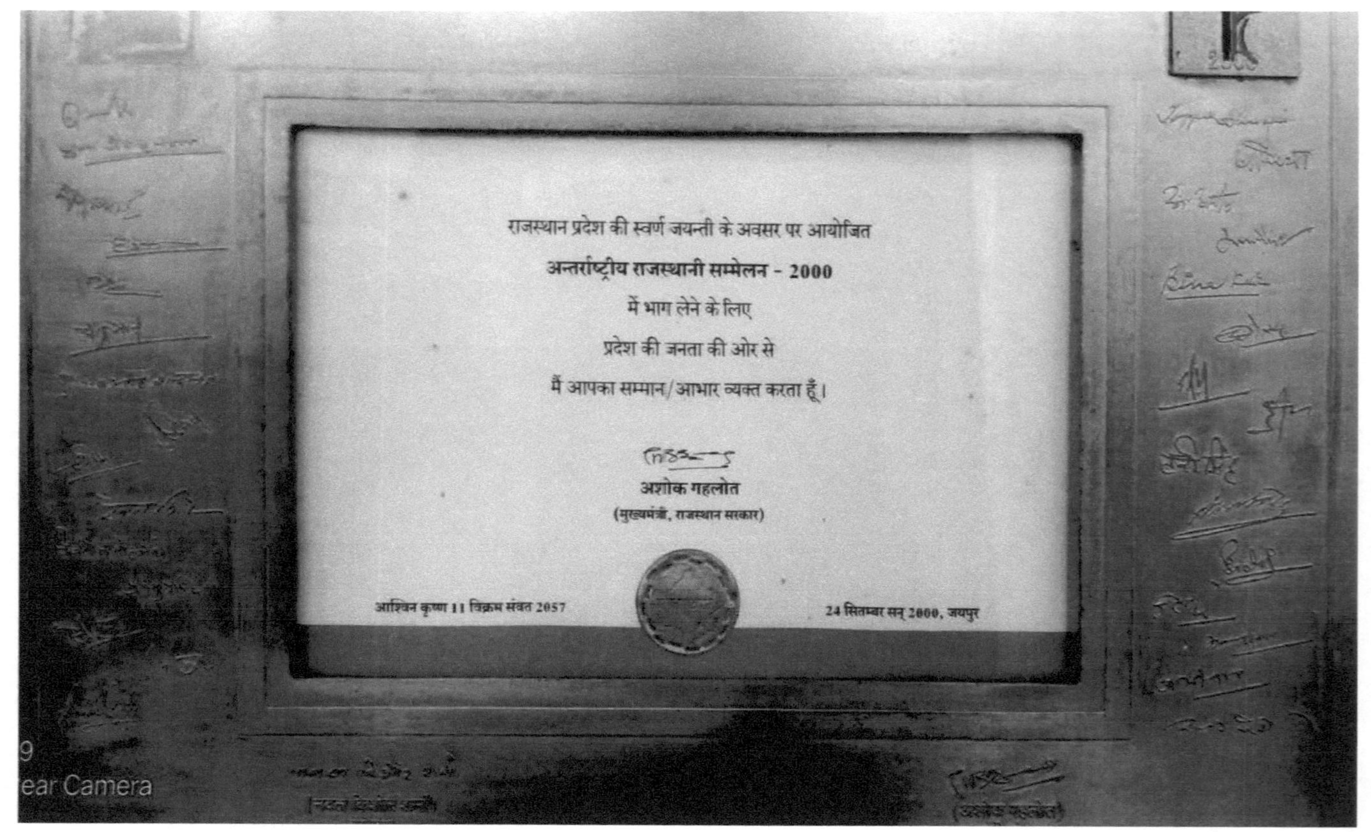
राजस्थान प्रदेश की स्वर्ण जयन्ती के अवसर पर आयोजित
अन्तर्राष्ट्रीय राजस्थानी सम्मेलन – 2000
में भाग लेने के लिए
प्रदेश की जनता की ओर से
मैं आपका सम्मान/आभार व्यक्त करता हूँ।

अशोक गहलोत
(मुख्यमंत्री, राजस्थान सरकार)

आश्विन कृष्ण 11 विक्रम संवत 2057
24 सितम्बर सन् 2000, जयपुर

पूर्वोत्तर प्रदेशीय मारवाड़ी सम्मेलन
(अखिल भारतवर्षीय मारवाड़ी सम्मेलन की प्रादेशिक इकाई)
39, वृन्दावन मार्केट, पहला तल्ला, एस. जे. रोड, आठगाँव, गुवाहाटी - 781001, असम
आजीवन सदस्य
MURALI DHAR KHAITAN
(मारवाड़ी सम्मेलन, जोरहाट शाखा)
आजीवन सदस्यता क्रमांक : PMS/KHA/05/0016
को
अखिल भारतवर्षीय मारवाड़ी सम्मेलन की
आजीवन सदस्यता प्रदान करते हुए हमें अपार प्रसन्नता
हो रही है। पूर्वोत्तर प्रदेशीय मारवाड़ी सम्मेलन आपके
उज्ज्वल भविष्य की कामना करता है।
धन्यवाद।
(मधुसूदन सीकरिया)
प्रांतीय अध्यक्ष
(राज कुमार तिबाड़ी)
प्रांतीय महामंत्री
(संजय कुमार मोर)
प्रांतीय कोषाध्यक्ष
(कृष्ण कुमार जालान)
प्रांतीय संगठन मंत्री
दिनांक :
2 अक्टुबर, 2019, बुधवार

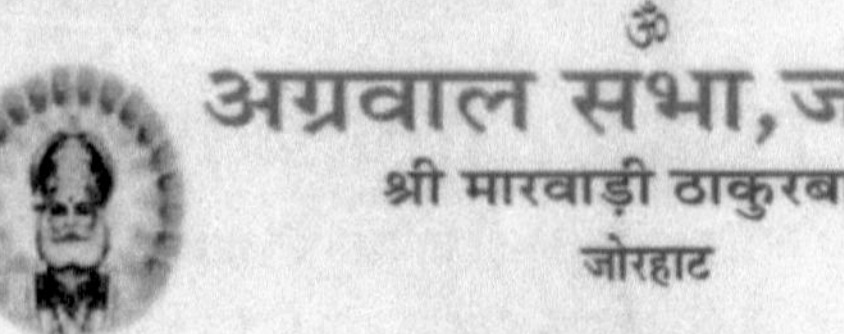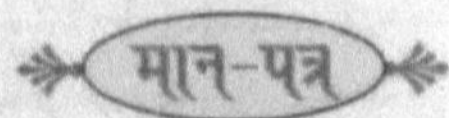

ॐ

अग्रवाल सभा, जोरहाट

श्री मारवाड़ी ठाकुरबाड़ी

जोरहाट

मान-पत्र

सादगी, शालीनता एवं सरलता का पर्यायवाची नाम है श्री मुरलीधर खेतान। हँसमुख, मृदुभाषी, उदार हृदय की प्रतिमूर्ति है श्री मुरलीधर खेतान। याचक के सम्मुख समर्पण के साथ-साथ इनके चेहरे पर निःस्वार्थ भाव की मुस्कुराहट देख निम्नलिखित पंक्तियाँ बरबस स्मरण हो आती है -

देन हार कोई और है देवत है दिन रैन।
लोग भरम हम पर करें ता से नीचे नैन ॥

किसी भी परिस्थिति में आपकी सकारात्मक सोच के कारण ही आज आपका नाम उद्योग जगत में कई ऊँचाइयों को छू रहा है, इसका जीता जागता उदाहरण है ३० अगस्त २००८ को देश के प्रधान मंत्री डा॰ मनमोहन सिंह द्वारा आपकी निष्ठा, लगन एवं कर्मठता का पारितोषिक स्वरूप उद्योग जगत में उत्कृष्ट प्रदर्शन के लिए आपको सूक्ष्म, लघु एवं मध्यम उद्यम मंत्रालय का **उत्कृष्ट उद्यमिता प्रयास राष्ट्रीय पुरस्कार २००७** प्रदान किया गया।

अनेक संस्थाओं से आपका जुड़ाव आपकी सामाजिकता एवं मिलनसारीता को दर्शाता है। शहर में आर्थिक सहयोग प्रदान करने वालों में आपका नाम अग्रिम पंक्ति में लिया जाता है।

अग्रवाल सभा आपके उज्ज्वल भविष्य के साथ-साथ आपके कृतित्व की कीर्ति सदा धवल बनी रहने की कामना करती है। **अग्रसेन जयंती** के पावन अवसर पर अग्रवाल सभा आपको यह **मान-पत्र** प्रदान करते हुए अपने आपको गौरवान्वित महसूस करती है। आपके स्वस्थ शरीर एवं दीर्घायु की कामना के साथ ...

मुख्य न्यासी
अग्रवाल सभा, जोरहाट
(भगवती प्रसाद गोयल)

अध्यक्ष
अग्रवाल सभा, जोरहाट
(रामावतार अग्रवाल)

सचिव
अग्रवाल सभा, जोरहाट
(कृष्ण बजाज)

ॐ जय श्री राम

श्री गीता आश्रम Shree Geeta Asharm श्री गीता आश्रम

SHREE GEETA GAUSHALA PARAMARTH SANSTHA (TRUST)

N.H. - 37, Podumoni (500 mtrs. from Kenduguri By Pass)

A. T. Road, Jorhat- 785010 (Assam)

E-mail : omjaishriram@yahoo.com

Cell : 94350 90285, 7002959522

Ref No...........   Date:.....**01–06–2020**

प्रमाण पत्र

श्री मुरलीधर जी खेतान

सेउनीआली, जोरहाट

श्री गीता गौशाला परमार्थ संस्था (ट्रष्ट) के ट्रष्ट बोर्ड के प्रस्ताव अनुसार इस ट्रष्ट का आजीवन ट्रष्टी बनने के लिए आपकी स्वीकृति मिलने से हम आपके आभारी हैं।

ट्रष्ट बोर्ड द्वारा यह घोषित और प्रमाणित किया जाता है कि आज दिनांक 1 जून 2020, सोमवार से श्री मुरलीधर जी खेतान जोरहाट ट्रष्ट के आजीवन ट्रष्टी नियुक्त किये गये हैं।

आपकी आजीवन ट्रष्टीशिप (न्यासिता) आज से आजीवन बलवत है। हम आशा करते हैं कि आपके मार्गदर्शन से ट्रष्ट का परमार्थिक कार्य उत्तरोत्तर प्रगति करेगा। आपके सुस्वास्थ्य व शुभ कामनाओं के साथ आपका हार्दिक अभिनंदन है।

ट्रष्ट बोर्ड की ओर से

हनुमान प्रसाद बाहेती

प्रबंधक न्यासी

जोरहाट   वास्ते, श्री गीता गौशाला परमार्थ संस्था (ट्रष्ट)

दिनांक: 01 जून 2020   पदुमनी, जोरहाट (असम)

॥ ॐ जय श्री राम ॥

श्री गीता आश्रम Shree Geeta Asharm श्री गीता आश्रम

SHREE GEETA GAUSHALA PARAMARTH SANSTHA (TRUST)

N.H. - 37, Podumoni (500 mtrs. from Kenduguri By Pass)
A. T. Road, Jorhat- 785010 (Assam)
E-mail : omjaishriram@yahoo.com
Cell : 94350 90285, 7002959522

Ref No...   Date: 01-06-2020

◇ प्रमाण पत्र ◇

श्री मुरलीधर जी खेतान

सेउनीआली, जोरहाट

श्री गीता गौशाला परमार्थ संस्था (ट्रष्ट) के ट्रष्ट बोर्ड के प्रस्ताव अनुसार इस ट्रष्ट का आजीवन ट्रष्टी बनने के लिए आपकी स्वीकृति मिलने से हम आपके आभारी हैं।

ट्रष्ट बोर्ड द्वारा यह घोषित और प्रमाणित किया जाता है कि आज दिनांक 1 जून 2020, सोमवार से श्री मुरलीधर जी खेतान जोरहाट ट्रष्ट के आजीवन ट्रष्टी नियुक्त किये गये हैं।

आपकी आजीवन ट्रष्टीशिप (न्यासिता) आज से आजीवन बलवत है। हम आशा करते हैं कि आपके मार्गदर्शन से ट्रष्ट का परमार्थिक कार्य उत्तरोत्तर प्रगति करेगा। आपके सुस्वास्थ्य व शुभ कामनाओं के साथ आपका हार्दिक अभिनंदन है।

ट्रष्ट बोर्ड की ओर से

हनुमान प्रसाद बाहेती

प्रबंधक न्यासी

वास्ते, श्री गीता गौशाला परमार्थ संस्था (ट्रष्ट)
पदुमनी, जोरहाट (असम)

जोरहाट

दिनांक: 01 जून 2020

Mr. Murli Dhar Khetan Met me sometime in September 1991, soon after I had taken over as Chair of Assam Electricity Board. He was then the proprietor of the North Eastern Cables and Conductor and in that capacity, was the principal supplier of conductors to the Electricity Board. I Stayed in the Board for over three and half years and throughout this period Mr. Khetan impressed me with his impeccable integrity and superlative ability to perform. I was quite confident that these exceptional qualities would take his far in his chosen field as well as in other areas both in industry and in the service of humanity. He has not disappointed me. His achievements in his chosen field of conductors and cables has now enveloped multiple functions including turnkey projects in supply, contruction and commissioning of transmission and distribution lines. So much so, that in this field, Mr. Khetan has attained super eminent status in the north-east region of India. Not content with being confined to one industry, he has spread his activities into diverse fields of manufacture and marketing. However, what I am most impressed with, is the University that he has set up in Kaziranga, which today is counted among the preeminent institutions of its kind in the region. That according to my estimation will be the permanent maker of Mr. Khetan's achievement. Mr. Khetan is ninety years old but he has ahuge reserve of energy and enthusiasm within himself. I would like to see him devote a part of the energy and enthusiasm into taking the University to further heights and achievements.

I wish him well.

Hilary Pais.
LLB. PhD (Business Administration)
Indian Administrative Service (retd)

1st of October 2020

G H Hegde
General Manager {Retd)
Indian Bank
Phone-9483328395

#24,17thMain1stCross
BT M Layour 1st Stage
Bangalore 560068

30th September 2020

Dear Shri Khetan Ji,

It gives me an immense pleasure to know that you will be soon completing 90 years on 10th November and on this great occasion, a book covering your achievements and journey of life will be published by your family.

I was very fortunate to have been associated with you, during my tenure as Circle Head of Indian Bank North East Circle in Guwahati from 2002-2005, as your company was one of the topmost customers of our bank in north east.

During my visit to your factory and office I was very impressed with the way in which business was conducted and dedicated hard work being put in by you and your family members especially Mr. Jaiprakash Khetan and Mr. Basant Khetan supported by younger generation.

It would not have been possible for an ordinary person to venture into business in Jorhat at a time when north east was least developed and was not even properly connected through transport and communication. In such times you further entered into the area of manufacturing and started M/s North East Cables and Conductors Pvt Ltd in 1959, which has today became a big corporate spreading its wings to other parts of the country, diversifying into new areas and tie up with multinational companies. I congratulate you for your vision and taking the company to such great heights under your leadership.

I am sure that the New India which we dream of building will be reality with companies set up by visionaries like you and the enterprising team putting their untiring efforts to improve and grow further in all areas in days to come. I am sure, M/s NEC CON group will be one of the biggest contributors in this direction under your continued leadership.

Business apart, you have established charitable trusts for serving the poor and needy and also involved yourself in various social activities as you belive in "Service to MAN is service to GOD"

I convey my best wishes on this occasion and pray for your long healthy life to enable you to continue the service to the nation and society.

With kind regards,

Yours Sincerely

GN Hegde

To,

Dr. M.D. Khetan, Chairman NEC CON Group

JORHAT

H.R.Jain

502, Bhanu Vinayak
18th Road, Khar(W)
Mumbai -400052,
Date: 05.10.2020

I was elated to know that Dr. Murlidhar Khetan Saab is coming up with his biography and it is my sincere pleasure to write down a few words about him.

In my own personal experience, Dr. Khetan is an earnest man. He has always been down to earth and truly in every sense of the word, a thorough gentleman. It has been my pleasure to know a man of such brilliance for more than three decades. He is honest, hardworking, and a believer of the moral values of life. These happen to be just a few of the large number of good qualities that he is a living embodiment of. In his group of industries he has always opted to manufacture products of the highest standard. He is an industrialist who has treated his employees as part of his family and that happens to be one of the many reasons that he has been triumphant in his life's journey. His unpatrolled growth as a man, from scratch to such a successful industrialist has truly been spectacular.

After achieving many milestones in his own life, as a man who believes in giving back to the society, he decided to give to the society -the gift of education. And with that he became a true philanthropist. He built a university in the state of Assam where thousands of students are imparted education every year. This gives them the first step towards a glorious career. It is beyond any doubt that his biography will inspire thousands of individuals to work with perseverance and achieve success in their own lives. It wouldn't be an exaggeration if I call him a Kalpa-Vriksha of Assam under whom thousands of people fulfill their desires every year.

On the 10th November 2020, he will be celebrating his 90th birthday. With this biography he has achieved yet another milestone and I wish him a long, healthy & wealthy life with many more feathers in his cap. May God bless a man of such impeccable character.

H.R.Jain
President, Smita Conductors Pvt. Ltd.

M.D. Khetan - a living legend

Dr. LP. Sahewalla
Profesor
Assam Agricultural University
Jorhat-13

It was God's wish thatl had the opportunity to be acquainted with Shri Khetanji since, otherwise, by profession we were miles apart and there was hardly any platform for us to meet. However sometime during I 98 I. I had a chance to meet him closely. My uncle Mr. Gajanand Sahewalla was engaged to his elder daughter Smt. Saroj Khetanji was a well established and successful industrialist of Jorhat and my uncle was from a comparatively modest family. I recollect from memory that there was stiff resistance within his family. Besides, most of the established businessmen of Jorhat were also quite surprised at this matrimonial alliance. However, Khetan ji remained undaunted in his selection and went ahead with the formalities. It was his respect and faith in education that made Khetanji go ahead since he found a well educated counterpart for his daughter and thought that it was wise to forego all other factors. Today my uncle is a highly reputed senior advocate in the Guwahati High Court with sound financial and social standing.

This faith of Khetanji in education was there for all to see in various aspects ofhis life including in the upbringing of his own children. His vision and courageous decision to establish a prestigious educational institution may be viewed as only an extension of his deep faith in education and the importance of human resource development. Today, Kaziranga University is an elite university in entire NE India. His creative thinking was instrumental in all round development in broadly all academic spheres of this upper Assam city. Kaziranga University is a dream fulfilled for Khetanji.

I have observed Khetan ji to be an amiable, affable, cool personality leading a highly disciplined life and capable of taking the smartest of decisions. He has that intuition to face all challenges in a most positive manner and always comes out with flying colours. I have never seen him display desperation or distress even though he may be passing through a crisis. He always seems cool and steady in his body language as if he has no tribulations in life.

He is healthy in the truest sense. A man is considered to be healthy if he is healthy physically, mentally and socially. His disciplined life has paid rich dividends, as even at this age of 85 he is maintaining a sound health and is active. Khetan ji is an embodiment of a truly hale and hearty man. He is a societal man and seems to enjoy the company of people from all strata of the society. He is a great philanthropist of Assam in general and Jorhat in particular. He has always contributed handsomely to all organizations such as the Marwari Thakurbari, Nava Yuvak Manda!, Agarwalla Sabha and other organisations. He has regularaly given significant charity for the wellbeing of the society at large.

I wish him a long healthy, joyful and fulfilling life.

हमारे समाज में कुछ ऐसे वयोवृद्ध विशिष्ट लोग हैं जिनके प्रति मेरे मन में अपार श्रद्धा का भाव है। उन्हीं श्रेणी के लोगों में एक महान व्यक्तित्व हैं– श्री मुरलीधर जी खेतान। ऐसे तो मैं उन्हें बहुत वर्षों से जानता हूं, पर पिछले दस वर्षों से मेरा उनसे घनिष्ठ संबंध रहा है। महीने–दो महीने में एकाध बार उनका फोन मेरे पास जरूर आता है। राजस्थान से आकर नौकरी से अपना जीविकोपार्जन शुरु करने वाले श्री खेतान जी अपनी कार्यकुशलता, ईमानदारी, मेहनत और दूरदर्शिता की वजह से आज एक बड़ा साम्राज्य स्थापित करने में सफल हुए हैं।

तीन बेटों के परिवार को जिस तरह से इन्होंने एक संयुक्त परिवार में पिरोकर रखा है, वह आज के जमाने में एक मिसाल के तौर पर है। मृदुभाषी खेतान जी में समाजसेवा व दान देने की प्रति कूट–कूटकर भरी है। सचमुच खेतान जी की सफल जीवन यात्रा हम सब लोगों के लिए प्रेरणादायक है। उम्र के इस पड़ाव में आकर भी पूरे ग्रुप के व्यापार की वे धुरी है और आज भी उनकी अपने व्यापार पर पूरी पकड़ है। मेरी उनसे घनिष्ठता की वजह से मैं समझता हूं कि 90 वर्ष की इस उम्र में इतने अच्छे स्वास्थ्य की कुंजी है उनकी एक नियमित व नियंत्रित जीवन शैली, सादा जीवन और शुद्ध विचार और रोजाना दो घंटे दोस्तों के साथ ताश खेलकर कुछ खुशी के पल बिताना। कुल मिलाकर मैं खेतान जी को एक सफल और महान व लोगों को प्रेरित करने वाले व्यक्तित्व की संज्ञा देकर उनका अभिनंदन करता हूं और उनकी दीर्घायु की ईश्वर से प्रार्थना करता हूं।

भवदीय

डॉ. अशोक पंसारी

गुवाहाटी

01.06.2020

Betkuchi, NH-37, Guwahati - 781035, Assam (India)
97076-83013 / 0361-2270100 0361-2270400 registraroffice@rgu.ac : ww.rgu.ac

फर्म – लेखराज दुर्गाप्रसाद, राजगढ (चूरू)
प्रो. दुर्गाप्रसाद अग्रवाल (डाबड़ीवाला, पंसारी)

श्री कांजी रंगा विश्वविद्यालय संस्थान
जोरहाट के प्रथम भामाशाह – डॉ. श्री मुरलीधर जी खेतान

डॉ. श्री मुरलीधर जी खेतान का जन्म बानुड़ा (खुड) सीकर में सन् 1930 में एक सामान्य अग्रवाल परिवार में हुआ। इनके पिता स्व. श्री रामनारायण जी खेतान और माता स्व. श्रीमती सोना देवी खेतान थे। इनका विवाह 06 जून 1950 में हुआ और अल्प आयु में ही अर्थोपार्जन के उद्देश्य से आसाम चले गये। फलस्वरूप आसाम की राजधानी गुवाहाटी एवम् जोरहाट को अपना कार्यक्षेत्र बनाया और सम्पूर्ण आसाम में एक प्रामाणिक व्यापारी के रूप में प्रतिष्ठित हुए। डॉ. श्री मुरलीधर जी खेतान का मानना है "सफलता के लिए बाजार में वचन का पक्का होना बहुत जरूरी है, तभी लोग आप पर भरोसा करेंगे" यही आपकी सफलता का मूल मन्त्र है। आप व्यापार में साख सबसे जरूरी मानते हैं, आप मानते हैं कि सफलता की आँधी में भी कर्मठता तथा उत्पादन की गुणवत्ता से समझौता घातक होता है। कर्मचारी और प्रबन्धन के बीच दोस्ताना व्यवहार जरूरी मानते हैं। कार्यालय में कर्मचारी एवं अनुशासनहीनता आपको बर्दाश्त नहीं हैं, आप मानते हैं कि कम्पनी की सफलता में कर्मचारी का भी अंशदान होता है। इसी सोच की वजह से आज तक आपकी किसी भी फैक्ट्री में हड़ताल नहीं हुई, आप कर्मचारियों पर बेहतरीन खर्चा करते हैं, फिर चाहे उनकी लड़की की शादी का खर्चा हो या बच्चों की पढ़ाई का खर्चा हो आप सहर्ष अपने कर्मचारियों की सहायता करते हैं।

प्रारम्भ से ही माँ लक्ष्मी जी की आप पर असीम कृपा दृष्टि बनी रही है। आपने थोड़े समय में ही अपार अर्थ का अर्जन किया और उस धन का सदुपयोग सामाजिक कार्यों एवं जनहितार्थ करना शुरू कर दिया। समाज के हर क्षेत्र – शिक्षा, चिकित्सा, धार्मिक आयोजन, निर्धनों की सहायता आदि में आपका उल्लेखनीय योगदान रहा है।

आपके सादे और निर्भीक व्यक्तित्व को देखकर कोई भी आपकी महानता तथा आपके विचारों की ऊँचाई का अनुमान नहीं लगा सकता, दूसरों को आदर देना आपके स्वभाव का प्रमुख भाग है।

आपकी जोरहाट, गुवाहाटी, सीकर, दौसा में व्यापारिक इकाईयाँ है जिनको आपके तीनों लड़के इन व्यापारिक इकाईयों का संचालन करते हैं। आपका व्यापार भी आज तक संयुक्त है। आपने अभी तक रिटायरमेन्ट नहीं लिया है। आपकी कार्यकुशलता एवं जनहितार्थ सेवा को देखते हुए आसाम सरकार तथा भारत सरकार ने कई बार आपको सम्मानित किया है। दिनांक 30 अगस्त 2008 में भारत के तत्कालीन प्रधानमन्त्री डॉ. मनमोहन सिंह जी ने विज्ञान भवन नई दिल्ली में आपको अवार्ड प्रदान कर आपकी सफलता में चार चाँद लगाए जो कि आपकी सफलता का सबसे महत्त्वपूर्ण प्रमाण है।

ईश्वर से आपकी दीर्घायु की कामना करते हैं तथा आप अपने माध्यम से समाज को और अधिक ऊँचाईयों की ओर बढ़ाएं ऐसी ईश्वर से प्रार्थना है।

हार्दिक शुभकामनाओं सहित......

सस्नेह आपका, शुभाकांक्षी

दुर्गाप्रसाद अग्रवाल

डाबड़ीवाला – पंसारी

सादुलपुर (चूरू)

निर्मल भी हो सज्जन भी हो, सादगी का एक नमुना हो

मृदुभाषी हा मृदु व्यवहारी, मृदुता की गंगा-जमुना हो

जिस मुकान को हासिल करने में, कितनी मेहनत और त्याग

किया हे कर्मवीर कर्मठ-पुरूष। मेहनत से ही अनुराग (प्रेम) त्याग

हम गर्वित है आपकी गरीमा से, जो सूरज जैसे चमकती है

रोसन हमको भी करती है, जो किरणे हम पर गिरती है

शालीन सादगी, दया धर्म, हम स्वंम आपको मानते है

ये बातें कही सुनी ही नहीं, हम जन्मे हैं तब से जानते है

जिस कुटुम्ब के कर्मघार बने, उन सबको अपने साथ रखा

अपनो से ज्यादा ध्यान दिया, सहोदर हो या बन्धु सखा

सबसे प्रिय जो लगती है, सादगी जो स्वभाव में शामिल है

न्यौछावर है इस गुण पर हम, जो कर्मवीर इस काबिल है

देखा है फलों से लदा पेड़, नीचे ही झुकता जाता है

ईतनी स्वभाव में विनम्रता, कोई बिरलाही पाता है

हमारा सम्बन्ध आप से है, हम बड़े सोभाग्यशाली है

जुड़कर आपके स्वजनों से, हम भाग्यशाली है

है कर्मयोगी कुल के तिलक, कुल की शान बढ़ाई है

कुल-धर्म निभाकर के तुने, कुनबे को राह दिखाई है

है धन्यवाद उस ''जननी'' को, जिसने ऐसा रत्न दिया

कुल का नाम किया ऊँचा, ''मुरलीधर'' को जन्म दिया

जगदीश ज्यानकी-नाथ से, बस यही कामना करता है

जगदीश शर्मा द्वारा

समर्पित- श्री एम.डी. खेतान

श्री गणेशाय नमः

रामनारायणजी–सोनी देवी, अग्रवाल जनप्रिय खेतान।
सीकर राजस्थान के निवासी, खूड़ बानूड़ो जन्म स्थान।
खूड़ बानूड़ो जन्म स्थान कि, पुत्र हुआ श्री मुरलीधर।
पंद्रहवें वर्ष में विवाह हुआ, हुए सोहनी देवी के श्रीवर॥
    काम सीख कर करो कमाई, यह जगत है कर्म प्रधान।
    रामनारायणजी–सोनी देवी, अग्रवाल जनप्रिय खेतान॥1॥

श्री गणेशजी मनायकर, पकड़ ली परदेश की बाट।
लगे काम और कमाये दाम, कर्मक्षेत्र बना जोरहाट।
कर्मक्षेत्र बना जोरहाट कि, इलेक्ट्रिकल्स में नाम कमाया।
काजीरंगा प्रसिद्ध नाम से, विश्वविद्यालय चलाया।
    लक्ष्मी जी की कृपा रही खूब, पर नहीं तनिक अभिमान।
    श्री मुरलीधरजी सोहनी देवी, अग्रवाल जनप्रिय खेतान॥2॥

व्यापार बढ़ा संग परिवार बढ़ा, दो कन्यायें हुए पुत्र तीन
जयप्रकाश–रंजना, बसंत–स्नेहा, प्रदीप संग कविता प्रवीण।
प्रदीप संग कविता प्रवीण कि, गजानन्दजी सरोज के कंत।
उर्मिला बनी अशोकजी की भार्या, चिंता सब दूर करी भगवंत।
    बहुऐं आती तो बेटियां जाती, विधि का तो है यही विधान।
    श्री मुरलीधरजी सोहनी देवी, अग्रवाल जनप्रिय खेतान॥3॥

कर्मठ वणिक श्री मुरलीधरजी, दया–धर्म हृदय में धार।
श्रम–साधक और मृदुभाषी, सादा जीवन उच्च विचार।
सादा जीवन उच्च विचार कि, सुख–दुख में सर्व सहभागी।
चाक–चौबंद, अनुशासन पालक, नियमित नियम अनुरागी।
    वय के नवम् दशक में प्रवेश, वहीं दिनचर्या करे संधान।
    श्री मुरलीधरजी सोहनी देवी, अग्रवाल जनप्रिय खेतान॥4॥

श्री मालीराम जी याद कर रहे, शिवसागर में सराफ समुदाई।
श्री संवारजी, ग्यारसीलाल जी, प्रणाम भेज रहे छहों भाई।
प्रणाम भेज रहे छहों भाई कि, पावन शुभ घड़ी आई।
मंगलमय इस अवसर पर, आपको है हार्दिक बधाई।
    विशिष्टता संग शिष्टताधारी, "नीरज" जाने स्कूल जहान।
    श्री मुरलीधरजी सोहनी देवी, अग्रवाल जनप्रिय खेतान॥5॥

निर्धनियां यह जगत है, यहां धनवंता नहीं कोय।
धनवंत सोई जानिये जो, पर हित धन संजोय।
परहित धन संजोय कि, धन किसी का सगा नहीं।
धन से सबकुछ होय पर, धन जैसा कोई दगा नहीं।
    धन हो तो मन बांधिए, उपजै ना मन अभिमान।
    श्री मुरलीधरजी सोहनी देवी, अग्रवाल जनप्रिय खेतान॥6॥

श्री सांवरमल अग्रवाल
शिवसागर
(अभिषेक के ताऊ ससुर)

चलचित्र झलकियां

Dr. M.D. Khetan at Christian Colony to donate goods for children

Dr. M.D. Khetan in the moment of Inauguration of ATM of Indian Bank, Jorhat Branch

डॉ. मुरलीधर खेतान

Dr. M.D. Khetan in the moment of Inauguration of Mahavir Mill, Jorhat

Dr. M.D. Khetan casting vote in Marwari Thakurbari Election, Jorhat

Marwari Thakurbari lift inaugurated by Dr. M.D. Khetan

Elder Citizens honored by Marwari Sanmelan, Jorhat

डॉ. मुरलीधर खेतान

Dr. M.D. Khetan as Chief Guest in a programme of EKAL Vidhalaya

Dr. M.D. Khetan during EKAL meeting.

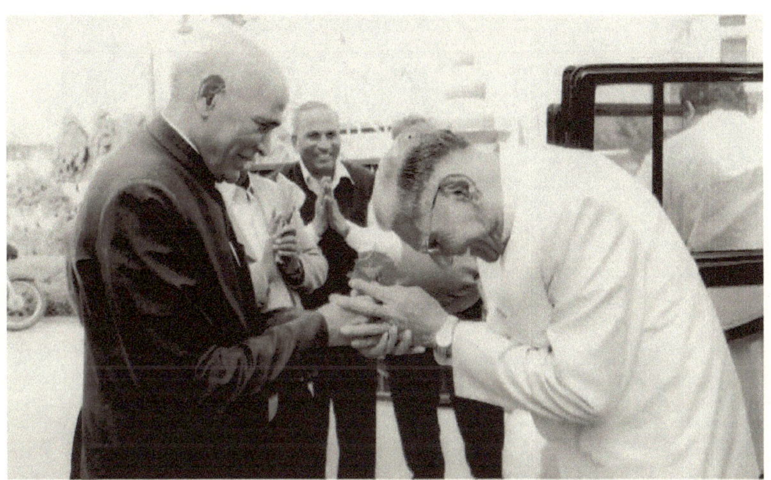

Dr. M.D. Khetan greeting Shri Rameshwar Lal Ji Kabra.

Dr. M.D. Khetan visiting EKAL School with member.

डॉ. मुरलीधर खेतान

Dr. M.D. Khetan is receiving "Abhinandan Patra" in Agrasen Jayanti Samaroh

Dr. M.D. Khetan during a meeting.

Dr. M.D. Khetan with his wife Sohni Devi Khetan.

Dr. M.D. Khetan during a meeting with Shri Tarun Gogoi.

डॉ. मुरलीधर खेतान

Dr. M.D. Khetan Mother Soni Devi during marriage of his son Jai Prakash Khetan.

Dr. M.D. Khetan with Bairam Jhakar.

Dr. M.D. Khetan during Award Ceremony in Jaipur Rajasthan.

Dr. M.D. Khetan

Smt. Sohni Devi Khetan

Dr. M.D. Khetan

Smt. Sohni Devi Khetan

एक परिचय

अंतरराष्ट्रीय स्तर के दिग्गज उद्योगपति डॉ. मुरलीधर खेतान का जन्म राजस्थान के बानूड़ा गांव के एक मामूली परिवार में हुआ था। आज वह करोड़ों केटर्नओवर की इलेक्ट्रिकल कंपनी निकोन पावर एंड इंफ्रा लिमिटेड के संस्थापक अध्यक्ष और पूर्णकालिक निदेशक हैं। उन्होंने इलेक्ट्रिकल व्यवसाय की शुरूआत जोरहाट (असम) से की थी। वह 1950 में महज मैट्रिक पास करने के बाद ही यहां आए थे। पहले नौकरी, फिर साझेदारी में इलेक्ट्रिकल उपकरणों का व्यवसाय, इसके बाद 1979 में हाईटेंशन इलेक्ट्रिकल्स के नाम से स्वतंत्र व्यवसाय की नींव डाली। चेष्टा, चेष्टा और केवल चेष्टा ही उनके जीवन का मूल मंत्र रहा है। उन्होंने काम के प्रति निष्ठा को नियति से ज्यादा तरजीह दी है। ईमानदारी, परिश्रम और सच्चाई के साथ कड़ी मेहनत करते हुए, वह इस उद्यम में सफलता की सीढ़ियां निरंतर चढ़ते गए। आज उनकी कंपनी भारत के पावर सेक्टर में सर्वोच्च शिखर पर है। तदबीर से तकदीर पर जीत हासिल करने की अपनी संघर्ष और सफलता की कहानी उन्होंने हाल ही में 90 साल की आयु में डायरी में दर्ज की है। जो बहुत ही प्रेरणादायक एवं पठनीय है। व्यवसाय में कदम रखने वाले नये युवाओं को निश्चित ही उनके तजुर्बे से बहुत लाभ मिलेगा।

तदबीर से तकदीर डॉ. मुरलीधर खेतान

www.ingramcontent.com/pod-product-compliance
Lightning Source LLC
Chambersburg PA
CBHW051221160726
47994CB00002B/690